A Basque Story Cook Book

*The tale of a pilgrimage from the Pyrenees,
warmed by flavors and fragrances from the
San Francisco kitchen of Martin's Español.*

by Ann Rogers

A BASQUE STORY COOK BOOK

A COOK BOOK FOR POOR POETS—And Others

Illustrated by
MARIAN EBERT

A
Basque Story
Cook Book

by ANN ROGERS

CHARLES SCRIBNER'S SONS · NEW YORK

Copyright © 1968 Ann Rogers

This book published simultaneously in the
United States of America and in Canada—
Copyright under the Berne Convention

A-9.68[nc]

Printed in the United States of America
Library of Congress Catalog Card Number 68-17347

To Miss G.

Acknowledgements

My deepest thanks go to Louise Abaurrea Dominguez, who so generously and tirelessly shared with me the story of her family and her mother's recipes; to Mamá, who—week after week—recalled each list of ingredients in the many dishes she had prepared; to Rita Rodriguez, who introduced me to *chorizo*-making and added several choice recipes of her own; to Rita's daughter, Stella Luyken, for her help; to Ciriaco Iturri, who presented me with a collection of Basque proverbs and their translation into Spanish; to Winchester P. (Chet) Wing, secretary of the California Wool Growers Association, who found a corner in his busy office where I could study facts and figures of the California sheep industry; to Elena Yparraguirre Gallagher, who added all sorts of Basque miscellany and was always there to answer a random question; to Norine Idiart Ward, who contributed her mother's favorite recipes; to Cecelia Dalmau, who added some of her grandmother's; to Dorothy Horst for impromptu assistance; and to Candelario and Pascuala Zalba and Joaquina Garcia-Baines, my wonderful hosts in Pamplona, Spain, who were responsible for so much I learned and saw in the Basque country.

Contents

The Story   THE RECIPES

A Basque Story Cook Book

❋ ❋

Introduction

Guernikako arbola, arbola santuba, adoratzen
zaitugu, arbola santuba.
Arbol de Guernica, arbol sagrado, te adoramos,
arbol sagrado.
Tree of Guernica, sacred tree, we adore you,
sacred tree.
From "Guernikako Arbola," the
Basque national anthem.

ASK A BASQUE the difference between a Vasco and a Spaniard
and fire will kindle in his eyes. He'll roar that there's a world of
difference! Proudly, he will tell you of the strength of his people and
their spirit—of their centuries of battling off invaders from their tiny
stronghold in the western Pyrenees. Sadly, he'll tell you how the beau-

13

tiful country of the Basques (but never their hearts) fell to Spain less than four dozen years ago.

❋ ❋

Who are the Basques whose homeland is the provinces of Alava, Guipúzcoa, Vizcaya, and Navarre in northern Spain?

Unrelated to other Europeans, the Basques are thought to be descendants of a late Paleolithic tribe. And, although it is now felt certain that they antedate the ancient Iberian tribes of Spain, their past continues to remain elusive. This mystery, which other ethnic groups might find disturbing, merely delights the Basques. "We are like honest women; we have no history!" they chuckle—only to contradict themselves in the next breath with stories of such noted Basques as St. Ignatius of Loyola, St. Francis Xavier, the South American hero Simon Bolivar, and Juan Sebastian del Cano, Magellan's first mate who took command of the fleet at the latter's death and became the first sea captain to circumnavigate the world.

Primarily a people of sheepherders, farmers, miners, lumbermen, fishermen, and navigators, the Basques are also keen and hardy warriors. It is said that, running out of gunpowder, they strapped knives to their rifles—thus inventing the bayonet.

Throughout the centuries, the Basques have probably resisted more invasions than any other people on earth. Successfully fighting off the Phoenicians, Romans, Visigoths, Arabs, and the armies of Charlemagne, they were able to maintain their independence until 1512, when their last remaining stronghold, Navarre, was conquered by Ferdinand the Catholic.

Until 1873 when they took a pro-Carlist stand in the Carlist Wars, and 1936–39 when they supported the Loyalist government in the Civil War, the Basques continued to be granted their *fueros* (local privileges) by the Spanish monarchs. Under the *fueros,* they were allowed to collect their own taxes—shunning arbitrary taxes on food, salt, and water; and

14

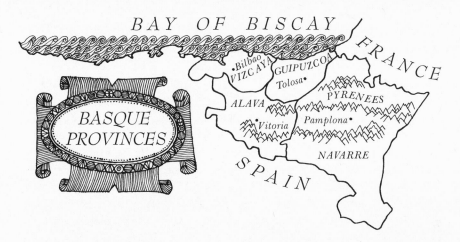

they were permitted to run their own local governments and resist military draft. They refused to sign contracts, believing that their spoken word was bond. All Basque affairs were decided by a council that met under an oak tree in the ancient village of Guernica.

But over the years Basque prosperity declined and, by the 19th century, emigration became common—especially to South America and the western United States. It is only in the last few years that the Basque country has miraculously boomed into one of Spain's most dynamic and economically sound industrial areas.

Through centuries of invasion, decline, near-collapse, and sporadic revival, the Basques have clung tenaciously to their archaic language, their habits of derring-do, their rich traditions, and their fierce loyalty. All summed up in the favorite toast of Navarre: *"Osagarria!"* ("Good Life!")

Like their predecessors, the beginning of their language is also obscure. It is an agglutinated, incomprehensible tongue which the Basques slyly call *"eskuara"* (clear). Some boast that it was the language of Adam and Eve; others claim that it was the only language to escape the Tower of Babel. But all Basques agree that the Devil himself once tried to learn *eskuara* by hiding behind the door of a Basque home. After seven years, he had mastered only a single phrase, *"Bai, Anderrea!"* ("Yes, ma'am!")—a tribute to the women of the country.

Although, for reasons of survival, the Basques have developed into strong warriors, they are—by tradition—pacifists. So it is reasonable to assume that the many Basque Separatist tricks—the bane of the Spanish police—are performed primarily for propaganda. Recent demonstrations of this kind include the substitution of a Basque flag for a Spanish flag on a Navarre mountain top, and the shooting of rockets from Pamplona's Plaza Mayor—each rocket releasing a shower of the now-forbidden Basque flags.

Like incidents have occurred ever since the beginning of the Spanish Civil War when the separate Basque republic, *Euzkadi,* was defeated. Although today few Basques support the Separatist movement, there is always a surge of pride and strong nationalism whenever a show of independence is reported. And they still look back to 1946, the banner year for Separatist demonstrations. That spring, only two hours before a championship football match, it was discovered that the huge Bilbao stadium had been painted from end to end with Basque flags and emblems.

A few months later, this time in San Sebastian (Spain's summer capital)—and on Franco's anniversary—the green and red Basque flag flew proudly from the highest pinnacle of Buen Pastor church. Harried police and firemen, taunted by the crowds that had assembled, worked three hours to remove the flag.

And again in San Sebastian, on the opening day of the regatta, hundreds of Basque flags made of wood bobbed in the harbor, upsetting, to an extensive degree, the Falangist show.

One of the most ancient of Basque traditions, that of honest smuggling, still flourishes today. Along the Biscay Coast, as along almost any coastline of the world, there is traffic in contraband items. But it is in the Pyrenees that the bulk of the smuggling is carried on. For a set fee, Basque mountaineers move men and merchandise over the border between France and Spain.

16

During the Civil War, they helped pro-Franco Spaniards escape the Republicans, helped international volunteers cross into Spain to fight for the Republic, and helped defeated Republicans flee to France. Then later, the Basque smugglers helped Allied aviators and fugitive Jews escape the Nazis.

Not long ago, the smugglers came to the aid of Secret Army Organization terrorists in eluding de Gaulle's police. And, more recently, they have helped Spanish and Portuguese slip into France to look for work.

All this smuggling is recognized by most Basques as part of their heritage; and they take pride in the fact that, although no contracts are written, the smuggled men or goods almost always reach their destination safely.

Other Basque traditions, less dangerous though no less colorful than smuggling, are within the law.

Basque men still wear the black *boinas* (berets) and continue to drink their wine from *botas*. These are the practical-to-carry wine bags made of goatskin with the hair side turned in and treated with tar. Basques claim that the *bota* gives wine a particularly good taste.

Drinking from a *bota* takes some practice. The technique is to start with the opening of the *bota* close to the mouth, squeeze to eject a thin stream of wine, and then draw the *bota* away—not losing aim—continuing a steady pressure on the bag.

The Basque game of *jai alai* continues in popularity. And, to celebrate special holidays, there are *aizkolari* (log-splitting contests), *kórikalari* (marathon races of men against trotting horses), and the ever-favorite folk dance—the *jota*.

Most of these traditional feats can be seen at any of the many fiestas in the Basque country today. But the most exciting and most all-inclusive celebration is the Festival of San Fermin. Every year, beginning on the seventh day of July, and lasting for ten days, the people of Pamplona celebrate their fiestas in honor of their patron saint, San Fermin.

There are impromptu street dances, prayers, bullfights, songs, fireworks, the municipal band, and numerous boys' marching bands. There are *gigantes*—papier mâché giants—and *cabezudos,* "big heads," to amuse the children and clear the streets for processions. All and everything at once and continuing, without let-up, day and night.

In all the gaiety and abandonment there is one event that draws the most participants and onlookers. This is the *encierro.* At seven o'clock every morning of San Fermin the young men of Pamplona race through the narrow streets with the bulls that will be fought that afternoon in the arena.

It is 6:30 a.m. and already the barricades, balconies, and windows along the 825-meter route are crowded with onlookers. As seven o'clock approaches, police clear the narrow streets of unwary tourists and the occasional comic; the crowds become hushed. Seven o'clock, and the first rocket is fired—the corral is open. A second rocket—the bulls are in the street!

Between the walls of the buildings surge men and boys in white shirts and trousers, hemp sandals, and red handkerchiefs. Their speed increases—the bulls are just behind them, overtaking them. Some boys roll under the barricades, some climb to protecting window ledges, some fall in the street and play dead. Some are caught on the horns of the bulls. But most continue to run unrestrained and without fear, for— during the *encierro*—there is time for neither thought nor fear.

In less than two minutes a third rocket is fired. The *encierro* is over. The sun is just beginning to touch the streets, the spectators come down from their balconies, and another day of San Fermin has begun.

❋ ❋

Of all the Basque traditions, one of the most delightful is the pride all Basques have in their food.

Every Basque considers himself an epicure. His home may be in the lonely sheep camps of the Pyrenees, the industrial throb of Bilbao, or the fashionable resort of San Sebastian. He may have an open cooking fire or a stainless steel kitchen. He may have a vegetable plot or a city market. But whatever his means, whatever his occupation—sheepherder, farmer, mill worker, merchant—each is equally particular about his food and its preparation. A visit to the Basque provinces is truly an adventure in good eating.

Meals are spaced relatively far apart but have many courses; the pace of eating is leisurely. There is good conversation on a variety of subjects, but the quality of each dish—the nuances of flavor, the crispness of the apple, the sharpness of the cheese—is always discussed.

The hour for breakfast varies with the occupations of household members. On farms or in fishing villages, the family will be at their kitchen table before dawn; in the cities, eight or nine o'clock is considered a more appropriate hour. Sometimes there is just bread to eat, but it must be the freshest loaf from the finest wheat. More often there are slices of *salchichón* (a dry salami) and the Basque sausage, *chorizo*. The meat is served sandwich-fashion between slices of bread or in fat soft rolls. Often there is a slab of *membrillo,* a quince jelly so stiff it is eaten out of hand, like candy. Always there are deep cups of *café con leche* (coffee with milk) or hot chocolate that's rich and thick as a pudding. And there is, hopefully, a plate of *churros*—hot crisp strips of fried dough sprinkled with coarse granulated sugar.

The Basque men often begin or end their breakfast with a small glass of whisky—the women with a sip of sweet wine. A pleasant introduction to the day.

For the visitor, the morning is a good time to drive through the countryside, admiring the ripening wheat, the fat sheep, and the pairs of yoked oxen protected from the sun by red-fringed hats of unsheared sheep or goat skin. The little fields make a patchwork of the rolling hills and, in the summer, there are wild red poppies and blue bachelor buttons bordering the roads and fences and splashing their color among the green grasses as far as the eye can see.

If your way is along the coast, the roads wind through forests of

19

pine and fern, dipping to the sea only where, centuries before, small natural harbors were formed in the otherwise sheer cliffs. Here, tiny villages cling to the rocks, and brightly painted fishing boats go out and return, their holds heavy with the day's catch.

Again, if your mood takes you into the Pyrenees, you will find scrub growth, jutting and precipitous rock formations, an occasional flock of sheep or goats, and cold streams where brown trout laze in deep pools.

Still another rewarding excursion for the visitor is a trip to a Basque market with your hostess—to wander from stall to stall, comparing prices and quality, swapping a recipe or two, while you fill a shopping basket and ponder important questions: Where is the crispest lettuce, the shiniest cucumber? Is it wise to splurge on the wild strawberries, arranged in neat rows in fern-lined trays? If you heap your basket with eggplants or melons, how can you possibly carry the meat?

So you move on to the meat section where the butchers, sturdy women in long white coats, are almost hidden behind the stacks of fresh and smoked meats and the sausages that festoon their individual stalls. One sausage has too much paprika. There, you can easily tell for it has stained the white paper on the counter. But here . . . here is a fine sausage. It soon becomes easy to tell the difference, you are told. Then you see and marvel at the legs of lamb—so young, so small, that each can weigh little more than two pounds.

Your last stop is the fish market. Here are women in bright oilcloth aprons and rubber boots. On trays of crushed ice, and with considerable thought as to composition and color scheme, they display fish and shellfish in infinite variety. There are neat mounds of mussels and clams, gooseneck barnacles, scallops, cockles, limpets, periwinkles, and sea snails. There are squid and eel. There is every size fish from slim anchovies to a tuna so big it takes three women to lift it. And there is row upon row of lobster and shrimp, each species arranged according to size and color. In front of the counters are crabs scuttling around in their string-bag or wicker-basket prisons.

Home you walk with your heavy basket, along tree-shaded avenues where the front of every house is an avalanche of geraniums and carnations. On through narrow streets with a canopy, high overhead, of wash hanging to dry. Out into the sun again, to pass shop after shop with windows brilliant from their meticulous daily washing. At last you mount cool dim marble stairs, saying *"Buenos dias"* to the concierge who maintains a shoe-repair shop in his little cubicle. Then, having un-loaded your basket in the kitchen, you start at once to help your hostess prepare dinner which will be served at three—the hour when Basque children come home from school.

Like the market of this morning, or your pastoral drives of other mornings, this dinner reflects the scope of Basque food production and the care given to their food preparation.

There is soup with fine vermicelli. The wheat, no doubt, ripened in the very fields that border the town. There are fat tomatoes, sliced and sprinkled with chopped fresh garlic and olive oil. There are boiled baby potatoes and green beans.

Almost every Basque eats fish at least once a day, and this course comes next. Sometimes the fish or shellfish is poached and the stock saved for soup. On special occasions, there are *anguilas* (tiny baby eels) from fresh-water streams. Again, it may be one of several exquisite white fish, gently sautéed in olive oil and butter.

And now—the meat course: a generous steak or roast, or lamb chops so tiny there is just one delectably tender bite to each.

Throughout dinner there is always wine; it is considered part of good nutrition. Vineyards dot the Basque country, and there is never-ending friendly rivalry as to precisely which region produces the finest grapes. One wine cellar stoutly maintains that the best wine is from the grapes grown in the Rio Jano valley, and so has its crockery wine

21

pitchers inscribed: *"Si el vino es bueno / y el jamón sano / no lo dudes es del Rio Jano."* ("If the wine is good / and the ham wholesome / there are no doubts it is from Rio Jano.")

Table wine is usually a claret or a rosé, the latter with decidedly more character than that generally available in the United States. Many Basques, the women especially, top their wine with a generous splash of carbonated water.

The table is cleared and you sit back, a bit drowsy now—warmed by the true Basque friendship, the conversation, the wine, and, above all, the fullness of Basque cuisine. But there is scarcely time for reverie. Dessert appears. It is a bowl of creamy rice custard, faintly scented with cinnamon, and followed by tiny cups of strong coffee. Then, no sooner than the coffee cups are removed, there is fruit and cheese and small glasses of brandy.

Afternoons (what little is left of them after dinner) and early evenings take on an understandably leisurely pace. For many it is necessary to return to work: to the field, where the peasant and his family labor on until after dark, or to the offices and shops that remain open until eight o'clock. But, if there is no business to be attended to, the remaining hours until supper (served at nine o'clock and similar to dinner, except with fewer courses) can be devoted to strolls in the park, coffee or a cold drink in one of the many sidewalk cafes, or calls on friends and relatives.

And it is during these visits that the idea becomes fixed forever that each Basque, no matter his economic status, is—at heart—an epicure.

You drop in at the cottage of family friends in the tiny Basque village of Aoiz. A broody hen is clucking in a box by the kitchen stove, a cow stamping restlessly in the stable below. The people greet you warmly with a kiss on both cheeks and a cordial *"Buenas tardes.* Welcome. Sit here. Sit here." And, in minutes, the table is covered with bottles of red wine, plates of white sheep cheese, a whole big *chorizo*— all homemade—and a loaf of bread still warm from the *panadería.*

The talk then is of food. Of the cheese of this house and how it compares with the cheeses sold in the local markets, or the soft cheese of Burgos that is traditionally served with a sprinkling of sugar. And, although few of the members of this household have ever been as far away as Burgos, each knows of that special cheese and just what makes it different from all others.

Wine is poured, glasses raised. The first sip rolls on the tongue and is slowly swallowed. All eyes are on you. "Ah . . . ," you sigh appreciatively "A humble wine that my father, himself, makes," volunteers one of the daughters. "No, no. Not humble. This wine is . . . is . . . beautiful!" The faces about you break into broad smiles, for these people know what you have just discovered—a description of this wine cannot be put into words. "So then, drink more—drink more. It is good for you. *Osagarria!* " The wine glasses (large water tumblers, these) are filled and raised, filled and raised. More cheese is sliced. More bread. More *chorizo.* And the conversation—which has run the gamut of politics, farming, reminiscences of family and friends now in America—once again returns to food.

Apparently you are not eating enough. Even though all that is left of the *chorizo* is the rind, the generous servings of bread and cheese have been reduced to crumbs, and several wine bottles are already empty. Shaking his head, your host says sadly, "The food of this house is very poor." "No, no!" you hurry to assure him. "In all of Spain—in the finest restaurants—never has there been a grander *chorizo!* " "But the cheese . . . ?" *"And* the cheese. *And* the wine. All are . . . how do you say it? *Magnífico!"* Which it is, and your Basque host knows it, though he delights in your confirmation.

You enter a luxurious living room on the top floor of one of Pamplona's newest apartment buildings. There are thick rugs and deep chairs.

You are no sooner seated than fine china plates are spread on the low table before you. There are tissue-thin slices of ham, fat green olives stuffed with anchovies, soft cheeses, and little rounds of bread. The toast

23

is drunk in cider champagne. "Do you like it? Do they not have it in America? Ah, then, you must drink more . . . and the ham . . ."

As in the cottage in Aoiz, the conversation sweeps easily from topic to topic, but inevitably comes back to food. Expert tips for the buying of ham. The name of the best local cheese shop. Preferred temperatures for storing wine and champagne. Special Basque recipes and rules.

※ ※

Yes! There is a world of difference between the Basques and any other people in the world. And there's a world of difference in Basque cookery—the extraordinary things they do with ordinary foods.

Imaginative combinations of simple ingredients: eggs and eggplant (*Tortilla de Berenjena*) . . . potatoes and green beans (*Patatas y Habas Verdes*) . . . fillets of white fish with orange juice (*Lenguado con Salsa de Naranjas*). All palate-pleasing, subtly seasoned so the natural food flavors come through. (For Basque food, like the Basque people, is honest, straight-forward.) All prepared according to generations of Basque-proven rules.

To know these rules, you must *be a Basque*. To learn them, you must *ask a Basque cook*. That's why we introduce you to the Abaurrea family in this book.

CHAPTER 1

Journey to a New Land

Aideak alboan banan ortzak aboan.
Los parientes estan al lado, pero mis dientes en la boca.
My parents are at my side, but my teeth are in my mouth.

Martin Abaurrea awoke as the warmth of the sun first touched the stone house. He lay still for a few moments, absorbing the morning sounds. From the left came the creak of iron as the fire warmed the stove; slow-rainfall pattern of his mother's feet; low chuckling of the coffeepot coming to boil; and angry hiss as the fire bit into a piece of pitchwood. Finally, the familiar scrape of metal against metal as the

25

handpainted breadbox, a wedding gift to his parents, was opened. Martin could not remember when the lid had ever fit perfectly.

There were sounds, now, from the other side: His sisters' voices—rippling tones, like the little stream outside. The squeak of their clothes cupboard hinges.

He listened, too, to the sounds below. Soft thumps as the oxen in their dark stable felt the coming of day and the need to be outside. Rattle of brass against leather as the horse shook his head impatiently. And snuffling of the mule (was his appetite insatiable?) hoping to find a bit of corn overlooked by his companions.

Sounds of a house awakening.

And, suddenly, Martin was vividly aware of them all—separately and together. He meant to record them in his mind forever. For tomorrow he would be in a strange bed in a strange town, and in only thirty tomorrows in a very strange (almost awesome, if one gave too much thought to it) new land—America.

Martin opened his eyes and sat up.

❊ ❊

The decision had been a long one. Though perhaps it had *really* been made without anyone realizing it, that day in 1898 when Martin was 18 and Uncle Cleto went to America.

All the relatives had gone to Pamplona for the farewell. And there were so many wagons assembled—the men in their black suits and red berets, the women in their stiffly starched blouses and full skirts—it seemed that all Navarre was composed of Abaurreas. And somewhere in the confusion of tears, laughter, and shouts of advice and comfort, Martin knew that—someday, somehow—he would be the center of a scene like this, he would be waving from the train, "Goodbye. Good Life. *Osagarria!*"

All the 25 kilometers back to Ezcay, Martin was silent and thinking, though inside he was about to burst with his new decision. The wagon rounded the last soft hill, and there was home. He looked up and caught his mother's wistful blue-eyed gaze and blushed with the realization that there were no secrets from her.

Life again became the routine and familiar. So that sometimes it seemed as though the decision had never been made.

Every day began with the morning sounds of the house. Then there was breakfast—thick slices of bread and mugs of *café con leche*. Sometimes, as when the sheep were to be moved to the upper pasture, there was a fat potato omelet, too, with enough left over to carry along for lunch. His father and his two older brothers often had a tiny glass of whisky with their coffee—especially in winter. And, eventually, Martin did too.

While his sisters and mother were busy upstairs, the men began the outside chores. First, there was the stable just under the house to be opened. The good-morning slaps on the sleek rumps of the horse, the mule, and each of the five oxen. The chickens to be unpenned, a feathery avalanche of clucking and crowing as all tried to be first to the fresh scattering of corn.

There was the clatter of shiny milk pails. Several of the ewes were always fresh.

On cold winter mornings there was pruning to do. There were the fruit trees, of course, but it was the small vineyard that lay behind the house that demanded special attention. The local priest said that Martin's father grew the fattest grapes and made the finest wine in the village. And Martin's mother, who could always discover where the men secreted the choicest vintages in the stable, was sure to have a bottle ready when the priest made his daily visit.

Spring was an especially busy time, for then everything had to be planted at once. On those soft days rows of potatoes, onions, cabbages, and cauliflowers appeared in the kitchen garden—a prelude to the kettles of soups and stews that would bubble on the stove throughout the coming year. The fields behind were sown with corn for the livestock and wheat to be taken in summer to the mill in Aoiz. Enough of the powdery sacks would be brought home to assure a steady supply of bread until the next harvest.

Spring also meant sheep shearing and driving the lambs to market.

Then came the long summer days and moving the sheep—as many as 200 head at a time—from the pastures behind the house to the lush grass in the higher hills. And hoping that one would not be so busy with the sheep that he would miss the Feast of San Fermin when bulls were run in the streets of Pamplona and—for a whole week—the town was a chaos of carnival spirit.

Late summer and autumn were a hubbub of harvest. Day after day the kitchen was steamy with preserving fruits. Behind the stable the storage room filled with jars and crocks—until one could only slip in sideways.

So each year passed. From time to time there was a letter from Uncle Cleto in America. He told of his work in the quicksilver mines near a tiny California town—Hollister. He told of the wonderful opportunities and of his loneliness—his wish to have one of his nephews join him. With each letter it seemed more likely that Martin's decision would be realized.

But one by one his sisters married and left the little stone house in Ezcay and his two brothers were called into the army. Because his father was now *sesentón*—which meant that he had passed his sixtieth birthday —Martin was exempt from military duty. Much of the burden, then, of working the land and tending the sheep fell on his shoulders. Although in the end, as becomes Basque tradition, he knew that the farm, the livestock, the house—and everything in it—would go to his oldest brother.

Often, after the livestock had been stabled and supper eaten, Martin would walk to Gorriz, the next little village almost exactly like his own, except that it had no church. Here he and his sweetheart, Angelita, would talk about his decision and hesitantly plan their life together.

So when the decision was finally made—when Martin's father called him in and said that he was really to be sent to California—it seemed more a dream than all the years of true dreaming had ever been.

Now no time was wasted. Letters shuttled between Hollister and Ezcay. Papers were signed and tickets purchased. A trunk, sturdy though well-worn, appeared as from nowhere.

A last look at the house that had become so familiar over his 24 years—a final nuzzling from the old horse and the sloe-eyed oxen—the gentle blessing of the priest—tears—"Angelita, wait for me. I will send for you." His father's hard hand gripping his—the wagons lined up at the station—the blur of red berets and starched linen—"Goodbye. Good life. Goodbye. *Osagarria!*"

❊ ❊

Miles of water—an endless land—a strange language. Then, at last, the *café-con-leche*-colored station and the big sign "Hollister"—the familiar face of Uncle Cleto. The warm embrace, the reassuring Basque welcome.

How different life became. Long days deep in the ground breaking up quicksilver ore and filling a never-ending line of steel carts. Evenings in the crowded bunkhouse: ceaseless rumble of miners' voices (would they never end?). Through it all, and mingling with "Angelita, wait—," one word—San Francisco—repeated and holding in it the ultimate promise. There, Martin felt, lay his whole future. There, in the beautiful city by the bay—not here in the dusty town of Hollister.

But how even to get to San Francisco when pick and shovel work in the mine paid only two dollars a day and half of these small wages was turned over for room and board. Why, at this rate, he would be an old man before he could save enough to set himself up in business in the magical-sounding city named for the good Saint Francis—and send for his Angelita.

Then, suddenly, an unexpected opportunity was presented to Martin. One day, while he was standing in a long line of men before a gaping mine tunnel, the foreman called him aside. "I've watched you now for three months, young man." The voice was gruff and Martin feared, briefly, that he was about to be fired. "We need another man to open tunnels. Choose yourself a helper, and the job's yours."

"Yes, sir!" Martin gulped in disbelief.

And so it was that he began earning the unimaginable amount of ten dollars a day at setting dynamite blasts and, with his helper, clearing new tunnels and shafts.

Each payday, then, for the next two years—after deducting the necessary amount for room and board and holding out a small amount for savings—Martin mailed the balance to his sister in Ezcay. And she, in turn, deposited it in the bank in nearby Pamplona.

Until it was 1907 and Martin knew that he had saved enough to begin an independent life in San Francisco.

And, with Uncle Cleto waving a rueful goodbye from the Hollister station, the painfully slow train ride began. The wheels' steady clacking no sooner started than the brakes' squeal signalled another stop. Gilroy, San Martin (which made Martin smile), Morgan Hill, San Jose, Milpitas, each station exactly like the other in its *café-con-leche* paint and black slate timetable. Until, at last, the train rumbled into a cavernous wooden building—a maze of tracks and trains, steam, soot, baggage trucks, passengers, porters, vendors, voices, whistles—the Oakland Mole. And, at the far end, a broad ramp, a squat ferry, and the smallest patch of open sky.

Once aboard the ferry, Martin pressed against the forward railing and looked out across the Bay. There was his city—his and Angelita's. His blue eyes gazed steadily across the water and, when the ferry gained momentum, the huge wheels churning a frothy wake, the city appeared to rise right out of the water and grow to tremendous heights.

As the ferry bumped its way into the San Francisco slip, Martin looked down at his hands, realizing—surprised—that he had been gripping the rail very hard. Flexing the calloused fingers so that the white would go out of his knuckles, and turning palms up, he wondered what work these hands would find in San Francisco. But there was scarce time to ponder the question; the gangplank was being let down.

30

Martin shouldered his trunk and, with three eager strides, was the first ashore. He marched right through the Ferry Building. His eyes swept up Market Street, promising to walk its entire length some day. But not now. He turned abruptly and strode north along the Embarcadero.

The waterfront was a wonder of wagons, drays, freight cars. Sweating stevedores grunting under the weight of barrels, sacks, cases. A team of Percherons—gleaming gray coats—shaking their harnesses and stamping their great hooves against the cobbles. Jogging Oriental goods carriers, loose black pantaloons and coats, their burdens supported on either end of long poles. Salt-tanned sailors; merchants in fine suits. Industry. Determination to rebuild the city completely from the ashes of last year's Great Fire. Martin liked knowing that, at any minute now, he would be a part of this.

At one point, a mountain of neatly stacked lumber all but blocked his way. Wondering at the pink color and sweet odor of the planks, Martin carefully detoured, and there was the most amazing array of food he had ever seen. Block after block of open-front stalls, each spilling its contents out over the sidewalk. Here, shiny green melons and fat round ones with skins resembling fishnet. Crates of apples, berries, and cherries. Bunches of bananas—fully as big as a man.

A noisy and pungent alleyway of poultry: chickens, geese, ducks, and here and there a turkey, its red-wattled head stretched high above those of the other birds.

Now, a street of vegetables—lettuce, spinach, peppers, peas— accented with brilliant tomatoes and carrots. It was the harvest of the little vegetable plot in Ezcay magnified one thousand times. And, suddenly, Martin realized that he was very hungry.

Time, then, to find the small Basque hotel his uncle and some of the men at the mine had told him about. It should be somewhere nearby. He would go there now and ask straight-out for lunch, a room, and—a job.

La Vaporina was a sturdy brick building at the corner of Broad-

31

way and Davis Streets. Martin pushed open the door, and somehow knew that he was home. The rumble of Basque and Spanish voices accentuated with quick laughter. The sweet smell that comes only from red wine in goatskin bags. The reassuring clatter of silverware and thick china in an adjoining room.

Unburdening himself of his trunk, he stepped to the long bar, extending his hand to the man behind it. "Good day, sir, I am Martin Abaurrea and have come from Navarre to make my home in San Francisco. I must arrange for a room and a job. But—first of all—a lunch."

The man behind the bar—one of the hotel owners—loomed heavy and dark. His eyes flickered over Martin. They saw a black suit that smelled faintly of camphor and bore creases clearly showing that, except for important occasions, it spent its time in a trunk. Worker's hands; one outstretched in greeting, the other clutching a faded red beret. And the haircut—as though the boy had done it himself.

"Hmph," said the owner to himself, and was starting to add, "A real greenhorn, this one," when his eyes met Martin's. Clear blue, like the deepest forest lakes, these eyes spoke for the man inside the Sundays-only suit: integrity, warmth, firmness, strength.

The hotel owner extended his hand. "Welcome. Take the last room on the right upstairs. Breakfast is at 7, lunch at 12, and supper at 6. A dollar a day."

"Good," agreed Martin.

"And, you want work—" the owner's hands flew to his temples. "Then why don't you buy this hotel!"

The men at the bar grinned. "We will discuss it," said Martin respectfully and ordered a glass of whisky—both as a toast to his new life and as a practical way of warding off hunger. For it was still 30 minutes to lunch.

That afternoon Martin walked up Broadway all the way to Russian Hill. Leaning against the rocky cliff, where Broadway came to an abrupt stop, he looked down the full length of the broad street. Hotels, taverns, bakeries, and grocery stores lined it. To the left—past imposing church spires—a hill rose suddenly and sharply, wooden shacks clinging precariously to its sides. To his right were more hills—these gentler— echoing faintly the sounds of re-building as the downtown area of San Francisco arose from the rubble and ashes of the disaster of 1906.

Why *not* buy La Vaporina? The owner had certainly not been jesting. Or had he? It would be fine to be the owner of a hotel—to stand behind the bar and greet the boarders each day—to walk from table to table during dinner, being sure that everybody had enough to eat and the wine-skins were never empty. To go to the produce market every morning and pick out the fattest vegetables, the shiniest fruit, the freshest eggs. To be at the wharf when the first fishing boats came in, ready to bargain for the best of the catch.

And more than that, to have a home for himself and Angelita. Oh, Angelita. He would write her today. At once. There must be no delay in telling her of their wonderful, their good life to come.

A cloudy thought: it was not possible that the owner had been jesting? No—that could never be. But, on the other hand, to think that it could! Martin almost ran all the way back to La Vaporina.

No. The offer—though bitterly given—had not been in jest. And, in a brief time, details were worked out.

All of Martin's small personal savings were handed over as a down payment. He had tried to hold back some, so as to send sooner for Angelita, but the owner had remained adamant. Martin did, however, have the job of bartender. Room and board, as well as a substantial amount toward the hotel purchase were always deducted before he received his wages. But, what little was left he carefully saved for Angelita's boat ticket.

33

Entremeses (*Appetizers*)

Bartending at La Vaporina, as at any Basque hotel, did not begin and end with the pouring of whisky or brandy or the filling of the soft goatskin *botas* with wine. It was the way of the men never to have a drink at one hand without a plate of food at the other. And it fell to Martin to see that the appetizers—the *entremeses*—were always fresh and plentiful.

ENTREMESES FRIOS (*Cold Appetizers*)

Aceitunas (*Olives*)

Never was the bar without a bowl of olives. They were usually green, but from time to time plump black ones made their appearance. On special holidays there might be olives stuffed with pimiento, almonds, or even anchovies.

Almonds and pinenuts were always popular, and the bar never lacked a bowl of one or the other. When walnuts, filberts, or peanuts were available, there would be baskets of these, too.

Cacahués (*Peanuts*)

Use canned or packaged salted peanuts, preferably the fat little Spanish ones still wearing their dark skins. Or have a big bowl of peanuts in their shells.

Almendras Tostadas (Toasted Almonds)

Packaged or canned toasted almonds are the most convenient, but home-toasted ones have a superior flavor.

Shelled almonds may be toasted, either with their skins on, or blanched. For the latter, put the almonds in boiling water, off the fire, for a minute or two. Rinse in cold water and immediately slip off the brown skins. Toast the almonds in a 275° oven for 30 to 45 minutes, stirring them from time to time. The almonds are done when they are crisp and a very pale tan throughout. Sprinkle olive oil and salt over them during the last minute or two of toasting, and stir gently to glaze.

Almendras Fritas (Fried Almonds)

Fry blanched almonds in enough moderately hot olive oil to just cover the bottom of a skillet. Shake the pan often. Sprinkle them with salt, and drain on paper towels.

Piñones Tostados Ó Fritos (Toasted or Fried Pinenuts)

Follow the same procedure as for almonds.

Avellanas Tostadas (Toasted Filberts)

Toast as for almonds, but omit the oil and salt. Instead, rub the toasted nuts in a towel to remove their skins and serve salted or not.

Nueces de Nogal Tostadas (Toasted Walnuts)

Although walnuts are commonly served raw, they are excellent toasted, and well worth the extra effort.

Toast walnut halves in a 275° oven for 15 or 20 minutes, or until they are crisp and slightly brown. Sprinkle them with salt.

Walnuts toasted in their shells have a distinctive flavor and are fun to crack and eat while they are still warm.

Leave the walnuts in their shells or, for easier eating, barely crack each shell. Toast them in a 275° oven for 30 minutes, shaking the pan from time to time.

Queso (*Cheese*)

Queso Roncal, the ewe's milk cheese of the Basque provinces, was not to be had in all of San Francisco. But La Vaporina boarders, big cheese-eaters to a man, munched happily on slabs of rather dry Monterey Jack. Today, cheeses to select from would be Monterey Jack, Muenster, or Greek Feta.

Salchichón (*Salami*)

Sometimes one of the Spanish groceries on Broadway, or across town in the Mission District, would receive a shipment of Spanish *salchichón.* Then Martin (whose bartending duties also included some shopping for supplies) would come home laden with these long, sweet-smelling salamis. At other times a very dry Italian salami, much easier to come by in the many little Italian shops along Columbus Avenue, was served, sliced paper-thin.

Jamón (*Ham*)

Asturian ham, the best known of the Spanish hams, was then—as to-day—unavailable in the United States. But ham the men must have. Martin, then, substituted Virginia ham, sliced very thin *with* the grain.

36

Atún en Aceite y Vinagre (*Tuna in Oil and Vinegar*)

This was a favorite Friday appetizer. Solid-pack, white-meat tuna was removed from its can and well drained. Then it was placed on a bed of chopped parsley, sprinkled liberally with olive oil, vinegar, salt, and pepper.

Camarones (*Prawns*)

On long afternoons, when the ships were in port and lumber from Mendocino was being unloaded along the Embarcadero, the Galacians (perhaps just a little homesick) would sit around the bar talking of home, squirting wine from their *botas,* and eating piles of pink *camarones*—the shells dropping nonchalantly to the floor.

2 pounds raw prawns 2 stalks celery
1 medium onion   1 tablespoon salt
1 clove garlic   8 cups water

Bring the water, vegetables, and salt to a boil, add the prawns, and simmer for 15 minutes. Allow the prawns to cool in the liquid, then drain them well and chill. *Camarones* are served in their shells, so have plenty of paper napkins handy.

Percebes Herbidos (*Boiled Barnacles*)

Rocks and wooden pilings, as well as ships, are the homes of these small crustaceans. Considered a plague by those who must scrape them from their ships periodically, the barnacles are, for Basques, a special appetizer. They are rinsed and boiled in water with a clove of garlic for 10 to 15 minutes. Drained and chilled, they are eaten from their shells.

Those living near the coast might well consider devoting part of a sea-shore outing to a barnacle hunt. But, for health reasons, a check with the Fish and Game Commission is imperative.

Anchoas (Anchovies)

Anchovies! The way La Vaporina's boarders went after them Martin wondered anchovies weren't packed in tubs instead of small tins. Sometimes there were plates of flat fillets. On special occasions there were anchovies rolled around a caper and fastened with a toothpick.

Sardinas (Sardines)

This was another easy appetizer, for all there was to do was open the tin, and dump the sardines—packed in either olive oil or tomato sauce —on a serving dish.

Huevos Cocidos (Hardboiled Eggs)

Sometimes the hardboiled eggs were halved, the yolks mashed with mayonnaise, salt, and pepper, and then stuffed back into the whites.

More typically, however, the eggs were merely halved and served on a bed of lettuce with olive oil, vinegar, salt and pepper sprinkled over them.

Frutas Frescas (Fresh Fruits)

When they were in season, fresh fruits, especially thin sliced melons (such as cantaloupe) or fresh figs, invariably appeared as appetizers.

ENTREMESES CÁLIENTES (*Hot Appetizers*)

Albóndigas, or small meat balls, were reserved for Sundays or holidays, which also meant a crowd at the bar. Usually, on these days, one of the hotel owners would work behind the bar with Martin. But it was never long before the owner was drawn away by some of his friends. Then it would be, "Martin, a whisky here." "Martin, another *bota.*" "What—no more *albóndigas?* Martin!"

And much as Martin enjoyed those little meatballs (and he rarely missed the opportunity of popping several into his mouth as he refilled the platter in the kitchen) it was many years before he could shake the notion that *albóndiga* was a synonym for Sunday.

Albóndigas (Small Meatballs)

½ pound ground beef
½ pound ground veal
½ pound ground pork
½ cup dry bread crumbs
1 egg, beaten
¼ cup milk
1 clove garlic, minced
1 small onion, chopped fine
2 tablespoons parsley, chopped

1 teaspoon salt
½ teaspoon pepper
flour
olive oil

STOCK
¼ cup dry red wine
2 tablespoons tomato sauce
water to cover

Mix together all the ingredients except the flour and olive oil. Mold into balls the size of small walnuts. Roll the *albóndigas* in flour and brown in hot oil. Drain well and drop into simmering stock. Serve hot, impaled on toothpicks.

The *albóndigas* may be made ahead of time and reheated just before serving. A chafing dish or electric skillet makes a convenient serving dish.

Albóndigas de Bacalao (Small Codfish Balls)

At Hotel La Vaporina, as in the Basque provinces of Spain, *Albóndigas de Bacalao* were not usually served as appetizers. Rather, they appeared as a separate course following the entrée. But, because this might prove a shock to American eating habits, and because they go so well with before-dinner drinks, *Albóndigas de Bacalao* are highly recommended as an appetizer.

1 cup shredded codfish	1 small onion, chopped
6 medium potatoes	salt and pepper to taste
1 egg	flour
1 clove garlic, mashed	olive oil for frying
1 tablespoon chopped parsley	Salsa de Codorniz (see p. 189)

Soak the codfish in cold water for three hours, drain well, add fresh water, the garlic and onion, and simmer for 20 minutes. Drain well and shake the mixture over heat to dry. In the meantime, boil the potatoes until they are tender. Peel and mash them. When both the codfish and the potatoes are cool, beat them together, along with the egg and parsley. Mold into balls the size of small walnuts, roll in flour, and fry golden in hot olive oil. Drain the balls well and serve with hot *Salsa de Codorniz* (Page 189).

Sardinas Fritas (Fried Sardines)

Sometimes a fishing boat would come in with a catch of fresh sardines. Then La Vaporina's cook would prepare the dish so familiar in the Basque provinces, frying the sardines crisp in olive oil and dusting them well with salt and pepper.

40

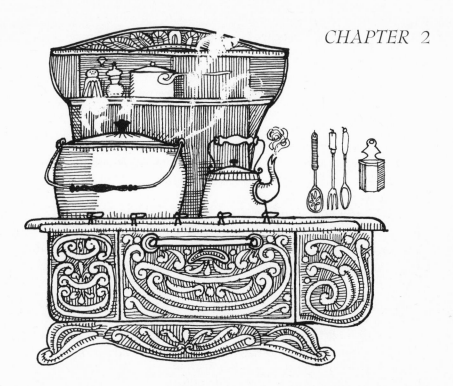

CHAPTER 2

The Lost Address

Idia aderra tik, eta gizona itai tik.
Al buey por el cuerno, y el hombre por la palabra.
You know a bull by his horns and a man by his word.

La Vaporina at last belonged to Martin. And a miracle of the saints that it really did.

For some reason that had never been made altogether clear to him (although he thought he understood it only too well) the hotel's owners had become, quite suddenly, impatient to sell.

41

"Now, Martin," as though they were addressing a child, "you *did* say you have sent much money to your sister in Spain and that she is saving it for you? Good. Now write to her and ask for your money. Then —like that you will own the hotel!

"But, of course, if no money comes—you understand—" a pause, "we must ask you to forfeit your down payment. It is only right, no? And, of course, we all know—because you said so—that your sister will send the money."

So Martin had written to his sister that very day. A month passed and he knew that she must have received his letter. Another month came and went and it was time for the money to arrive. Each day the hotel owners would look at Martin and then at each other and raise their dark eyebrows.

And still no word from his sister.

One morning the owners came to him. "Well, Martin, we have given you enough time. The money has not come. You must forfeit your down payment. It is a great pity, yes, but we can wait no longer.

"So—get out."

Martin's hundreds of backbreaking days in the mines, his thousands of tedious hours at the bar, his savings, his home for himself and Angelita, his dreams, his promises. All of these rushed together and tightened his throat in a hard lump.

Blindly, methodically, he reached for the revolver that he knew lay on its little shelf below the bar.

"No." He turned slowly. "No. It is you who must leave."

The men looked from the revolver's muzzle to Martin's eyes, unyielding blue as finely tempered steel. They swung on their heels, closing the door respectfully behind themselves.

Martin stared at the door. He became, then, conscious of the gun in his hand. He'd never touched it before today; it had merely always lain on its shelf, "in case." He wondered if it were loaded. Cautiously, he unlocked the chamber. Brass caps of six unspent bullets glinted up at him. As he replaced the gun on its shelf he realized that his hands were shaking and that his collar was sticky with perspiration.

After that day the owners treated him with courtesy and deference. Not another word was said about the money until the very day it arrived —as Martin knew it would—exchanged hands, and the hotel was at last his.

❊ ❊

And now it was March 24, 1911, a day in a period of time Martin had looked forward to so intently that it had never been necessary to mark these weeks on the calendar. Angelita had left Spain in February, escorted by her brother Segundo, and could arrive in San Francisco almost any time. Even today!

Seven whole years. And all at once it seemed a lifetime. Martin surveyed himself in the mirror behind the bar. Were there not now some lines, absent that day in Navarre when he had whispered, "Angelita, wait—"? Was some of his scalp showing through his hair—didn't his forehead seem higher? Wasn't his belt tighter? A bit of a paunch, hmm? Being a hotel owner was not easy, but neither was it like the rugged outdoor life of Ezcay or the equally rugged, though underground, mining life of Hollister. Was he getting soft? . . . Would Angelita even recognize him?

Martin felt very old and not a little depressed; this sort of reverie was not at all like him. Enough!

Noisily he set glasses out on the bar. The men would be arriving for their afternoon whisky. His eyes moved quickly over the room. Everything in order. He hurried to the kitchen to be sure the appetizers were ready. He was all over his brief waking nightmare, but couldn't help wondering, just once more, "Where is Angelita now?"

And where Angelita was was San Francisco—on a ferry boat to be exact—only a few minutes from docking.

It was a sparkling afternoon, the city looking much as it had on

Martin's arrival four years earlier. But Angelita was able to appreciate neither the beauty nor the excitement of arrival.

She had mislaid the paper with Martin's address.

She sighed a heavy sigh and again began the futile rummaging through her bag. "The United States," she announced to her brother, Segundo, "is a story of losings. It is now only the Dear Lord, Himself, who can help us find Martin."

"Angelita, Angelita, it is only the address that is gone. It is not as though you had lost the name of the city." Gently bemused, Segundo watched the search. "Now *that* would give us a serious problem," he added hopefully. He strove to sound reassuring but feared there was a hollowness in his remark. As the city came closer it became larger—as large as Le Havre, perhaps. With a strange new language, at that. And somewhere among these seven hills and sprawling buildings was Martin. Just how were they ever to find him? Where were they to start looking?

Angelita snapped her bag shut. "Well, it is gone. Yes, the United States has brought losses—but findings, too." She folded her hands in her lap, eyes sparkling up at her brother. "Never will I forget seeing you again in New York. Oh, dear Segundo, how good you looked—and strong. If Mama only knew," she giggled.

Patiently, wearily, Segundo heard the bafflement again. Angelita, separated from him on the ship—even before it had left Le Havre. "Travel on different decks? How? Why? But my own brother. Here are papers to prove it—it is not as if—"

The turmoil, bewilderment of Ellis Island: interminable waiting—checking of documents—waiting—questioning—official stamping. Waiting. At last Angelita was passed through a door, and she was really there—America. But what has become of Segundo? In the long voyage (the ocean was wider and more desolate than even she had imagined), in the long hours at Ellis Island—no Segundo.

Again Angelita waited.

44

"Bonjour, mademoiselle!" A young Frenchman before her gallantly swept off his hat. "Excuse me, mademoiselle, but I could not help seeing you earlier, in the customs offices. And now, that you are at last in the United States, you sit alone on a bench. You have no friends to greet you? Nowhere to go?"

He spoke so rapidly that Angelita was unable to translate every word. But here, at least, was someone who might help.

In moments she told this stranger of her childhood sweetheart in Navarre, her betrothal, her preparations for the trip. How her mother questioned her traveling so far. How Martin, now the owner of a fine hotel in San Francisco, California, could not leave his business to come back to Spain for her. How her older brother, Segundo, had been chosen to accompany her. And now—she had lost him!

"Well," decided the Frenchman, as soon as the tale was ended. "We will simply go to the train station. Your brother will be there. And —if he is not? You must get on the train—your ticket is in order, no? and I, myself, will be your chaperon until I must leave the train in Salt Lake City."

Angelita had no time to weigh the propriety of his offer, for the young man was already collecting her bag. "Santa Maria!" she whispered. And off they went.

Then a miracle happened. Or perhaps the Frenchman (unwittingly?) had been right, after all. There, on the far side of the train station waiting room, shaking his head, looking lost—and not a little angry—was Segundo.

"My brother! My brother!" Angelita tugged at her companion's sleeve. He dropped the bag where they stood and wiped his forehead. "Where, where? Are you sure?"

Again Angelita's voice rang out through the waiting room. Even Segundo heard her now. Relief softened his face, but—as he hurried toward her—he muttered "Women!"

❋ ❋

The ferry bumped the slip. "Well, we are here." Angelita and Segundo gathered their possessions, walked down the ramp, through a bleak corridor, between rows of dark wooden benches in a waiting room smelling of boot polish, fresh flowers, and fried food.

Out onto Market Street—blinking in the glare of late afternoon sun. Segundo set their bags on the sidewalk. "So?" he looked at Angelita.

Spanish voices from a little group nearby. Questions. Names. Street numbers. Assorted trunks and bundles. Angelita and Segundo turned instinctively, and a man—who seemed to be everywhere in the group at once—caught their eyes and strode to them.

"Ah, you are Spanish," looking at Segundo's beret he corrected himself. "No, Basque. Welcome to the City of St. Francis. You have friends—a place to stay?"

Once more Angelita told the story of losses, but this time held it to only the parts about Martin and the mislaid address. Segundo stood, silently detached, at her side.

Their new friend grasped the situation immediately and, though he did not say it in as many words, his brown eyes acknowledged that this was not an uncommon occurrence.

So it was decided. Angelita and Segundo would join his group, go to one of several Spanish hotels he knew, and from there—he was without doubt—they would find Martin.

The travelers—there were about six of them, some friendless, others misplaced—took up positions behind the stranger who knew the locations of Spanish hotels. As they set off, though it was pavement—not meadow—Angelita was reminded of Navarre and the flocks of sheep who would docilely follow the goat with the big brass bell, simply because he seemed to be the only one who knew where he was going. And how, too, the sheep would follow the Judas goat— She shivered at this thought and concentrated on her surroundings.

The little group was walking, now, along the Embarcadero—the wharves with their many ships on the right. After four blocks they turned abruptly to the left, into a wide street that rose gently into the setting sun.

One, two blocks. A corner marked by a squat brick building, crisp curtains at the upstairs windows. "Why—there—there. I'm most certain. There is Martin's hotel." They were opposite the building now. Angelita looked up at Segundo to tell him of her remarkable discovery. Now the little hotel was behind them. "Segundo—" His face was very tired and stern, and he barely heard her. "It is nothing," Angelita murmured.

Six more blocks. A wide cross-street whose shops bore names like Salvatore's, Guiseppe's, and Giovanni's. Windows draped with salamis, cheeses, and ropes of garlic, or piled high with crusty breads fashioned into long loaves, rings, sticks, and fat rolls.

Another short block, and a narrow street opened to the left. Roofs, their red or green painted corners ending in great skyward-swooping curves, shaded all manner of fruits, vegetables, and poultry set in crates before store fronts. The crates so filled the sidewalks that the people had spilled over into the street. Men, many very old, with long, wispy gray beards and little black skull caps on their heads, women in loose black silk jackets over straight pantaloons that almost touched the ground, and children—never had Angelita seen so many children—with round smooth faces, button noses, and eyes like almonds left too long on the fire.

Two more blocks and the group finally came to a halt in front of a small building, the sign above the door announcing that this was the Lugea Hotel.

Their guide singled out Angelita and Segundo and pushed open the door. They were in a long, somewhat bare room—a worn bar stretching down the entire length of one wall, round tables and chairs arranged along the other.

Once more, the story of the misplaced address.

47

No. No one presently here knew Martin. But, yes, there was no doubt that he would be found. No, the bartender was, himself, new in San Francisco. And the other guests? No, this was the only hotel they ever came to. But do not worry. When the owner returned—he, of course, would know precisely what to do.

"Thank you." "Do not fear—" "Goodbye." *"Osagarria."* And the young man who had befriended them outside the Ferry Building—the young man who was so kind to newcomers—still a stranger, was gone.

The room whirled. Angelita sat down. She closed her eyes. She opened them in a moment. There before her stood a young woman wearing a wide-brimmed velvet hat; its crown festooned with roses, a little fox fur around her neck, and carrying—of all things—a baby. Angelita blinked. What a strange country this is, where a lady wears a fine hat and fur yet has no maid to carry her baby!

Deep warm eyes. Reassuring words. "Yes," her husband was the owner of this hotel. Of course he would know Martin. "As soon as he returns—the telephone—and Martin will be found. You are tired. A cup of chocolate—a cake."

It was at least another hour before Martin was located and arrived, somewhat breathless and suddenly a little shy.

The story of the lost Segundo—of the lost address—of walking, finally, right across the street from and right past Martin's own hotel. Segundo's expression was stoic. But Martin's blue eyes gave away his amusement and joy, though he tried to make his voice especially stern.

"Angelita, as soon as we get to La Vaporina—you shall see. I will tie your apron strings to the stove, and never never again will you become lost. This I promise you."

* *

It was well over a month before Martin and Angelita were married, and Martin could keep his promise. There were, in the meantime, papers to be signed, documents to be filed. Angelita sometimes felt that the whole process of coming to America and becoming Martin's wife was wholly dependent on signing her name on the right piece of paper in the right sequence.

When she was not signing papers, Angelita was composing letters to Segundo—who had left after only two days in San Francisco to find work at the mines in Hollister, and to her mother in Gorriz. And—more important—she was learning the ways of La Vaporina's kitchen.

For, upon her marriage to Martin, the kitchen would come under her full-time direction.

Sopas (Soups)

At La Vaporina, as in most Basque homes, soup was served at both lunch and dinner. Furthermore, many of the soups were made from a basic stock of short ribs and vegetables. These facts no doubt explain why Angelita's soup stock recipe calls for a veritable cauldron—as well as a large family or a sizeable refrigerator for storage. (The stock will keep well for four or five days.)

So, for those who want *lots* of soup, here is Angelita's basic recipe. Smaller quantities are quite simple: merely divide the recipe proportionately.

El Caldo de Carne de Angelita (Angelita's Beef Stock)

2 gallons cold water	3 stalks celery
3 pounds short ribs	1 bunch parsley
1 large onion	2 tomatoes or 2 tablespoons tomato sauce
2 cloves garlic	2 whole cloves (optional)
3 carrots	salt and pepper to taste

Put the short ribs and water in a large pot. When this begins to boil, skim any foam from the top until the liquid is clear. Now add the vegetables, that have been cut in large pieces, and the parsley—well-tied. The cloves, salt, and pepper go in at this time, too. Cover the pot and let the stock simmer gently for 2½ to 3 hours.

Now cool the stock, discard the vegetables, and skim excess fat. Reserve the short ribs, for they can be eaten either cold, heated with *Salsa de Codorniz* (page 189), or simmered with potatoes, cabbage, and a little soup stock.

Sometimes Angelita cooked a cup or two of *garbanzos,* that had been soaked in cold water overnight, with the stock. They were removed at the end of the cooking period and served separately.

El Caldo de Gallina de Angelita (*Angelita's Chicken Broth*)

Another basic soup stock, *Caldo de Gallina,* can be used instead of beef stock for a number of soups. However, it is usually served clear or with a little rice.

The cooked chicken is served separately.

2 pounds stewing chicken	2 carrots
2 stalks celery	1 whole clove
1 medium onion	salt and pepper
2 cloves garlic	1½ gallons water

Cut the chicken in half and the vegetables in large pieces. Cover them with cold water in a large soup kettle. When the stock comes to a boil, reduce the heat and simmer gently for approximately 2 hours. Remove and reserve the chicken; strain the stock and discard the vegetables and clove.

SOPAS DE VERDURAS (*Vegetable Soups*)

Sopa de Verduras (*Vegetable Soup*)

1 or 2 cups vegetables (see below)   salt and pepper
4 cups Angelita's Beef Stock (page 49)

Almost any vegetables, or a combination of vegetables such as celery, carrots, leeks, spinach, chard, cabbage, or turnips, can be used. Chop the vegetables fine and add them to the stock. Cover and simmer one half-hour. (Leftover beans or *garbanzos* are excellent added to vegetable soup.) Serves 4–6.

Sopa de Verduras Fritas (*Fried Vegetable Soup*)

1 or 2 cups vegetables (see   2 teaspoons tomato sauce
  preceding recipe)   4 cups Angelita's Beef Stock
1 tablespoon olive oil   (page 49)
1 tablespoon flour   salt and pepper

Chop the vegetables fine and fry them in the olive oil until they are limp. Stir in the flour and continue frying until the mixture is golden. Now stir in the tomato sauce and soup stock. Season gently and allow the soup to simmer for a half-hour. Serves 4–6.

Puré de Verduras (*Vegetable Purée*)

2 medium potatoes   4 cups Angelita's Beef Stock (page 49)
3 good-sized carrots   salt and pepper

51

Peel and cut up the potatoes and carrots and simmer them until tender in the stock. Purée, season with a little salt and pepper, and serve. Serves 4–6.

Puré de Patatas (Purée of Potatoes)

4 medium potatoes
½ cup minced onion
2 tablespoons minced parsley
1 tablespoon olive oil
4 cups Angelita's Beef Stock

or Chicken Broth (pages 49, 50)
salt and pepper
croutons or small pieces of
toasted bread

Peel, quarter, boil, and mash the potatoes. Mince the onion and fry it in olive oil until it is golden, adding the parsley—also minced—the last minute or two. Add the vegetables, along with the stock, to the potatoes and simmer until the soup is well-heated. Season with salt and pepper and serve with croutons. Serves 4–6.

Porrosalda (Potato Leek Soup)

4 slices bacon
¾ cube butter (3 ounces)
6 medium potatoes
1 bunch leeks
3 stalks celery
1 large clove garlic
2 tablespoons minced parsley

2 tablespoons flour
1 bay leaf
1½ gallons Angelita's Beef
  Stock, Chicken Broth
  (pages 49, 50), or water
1 teaspoon white pepper
salt to taste

Dice the bacon and fry it in a large soup pot until it is just crisp. Add the butter along with the diced potatoes and sliced vegetables. Continue cooking—and stirring—until the vegetables are a little soft.

Sprinkle in the flour and stir until the mixture is golden. Now pour in the broth and bring the soup to a boil. Add the bay leaf, parsley, salt, and pepper. Cover and simmer 1½ to 2 hours. Check for seasoning just before serving. Serves 10–12.

Sopa de Cebolla (Onion Soup)

4 medium onions
2 tablespoons olive oil
1 tablespoon flour
4 cups Angelita's Beef Stock

or Chicken Broth (pages 49, 50)
salt and pepper
croutons or small pieces of
   toasted bread

Peel the onions and slice them as thinly as possible. Fry them gently in olive oil in a large soup pot until they are golden. Add the flour and continue frying for a minute or two. Don't let the mixture brown! Now add the broth and the salt and pepper. Bring the soup to a boil and then turn down the flame. Cover the pot and simmer the soup for one half-hour. Serves 3–4.

Sopa de Cebolla can be served strained or with the onions left in. Always it is topped with croutons or toasted bread.

Sometimes Angelita varied the soup by adding a tablespoon of tomato sauce and one whole clove with the stock. The clove is removed before serving.

Puré de Lentejas (Purée of Lentils)

This is a basic recipe that can be used with equal success not only with lentils, but with either *garbanzos* (that have first been soaked overnight in warm water with a teaspoon of salt) or with split peas. If the former are used, the soup becomes *Puré de Garbanzos;* if the latter, *Puré de Guisantes.*

53

2 cups dried lentils
1 teaspoon salt
1 small onion
1 clove garlic
1 tablespoon olive oil

salt and pepper
12 cups Angelita's Beef Stock
   (page 49), or water
croutons

Soak the lentils overnight in water to cover and 1 teaspoon salt. Drain and add to the stock. Simmer gently for one hour. Press the lentils through a sieve or whirl them in a blender. Now mince the onion and garlic and fry in olive oil until the vegetables are golden. Add the vegetables to the purée, cover, and simmer an additional half-hour. Taste for seasoning. Serve with a sprinkling of croutons. Serves 6–8.

Sopa de Fideo (Vermicelli with Soup Stock)

Like *Puré de Lentejas, Sopa de Fideo* is a basic sort of soup. Instead of vermicelli, rice can be used; in which case the soup is *Sopa de Arroz.* Or, if macaroni or alphabet paste is used, it becomes *Sopa de Macarrones.*

1 quart Angelita's Beef Stock
   or Chicken Broth (pages 49, 50)
1 teaspoon tomato sauce

½ cup vermicelli
salt and pepper

Bring the stock to a boil and stir in the tomato sauce and vermicelli. Lower the heat and cover the pot. Let the soup simmer 15 minutes, or until the vermicelli is tender. Season to taste before serving. Serves 3–4.

Caldo Borracho (Drunken Soup)

Although the Basques are notorious for their ability to drink and drink without ever becoming drunk, this—literally—is "hangover soup." Of course, if one feels merely "unwell," the dish may be called by its more righteous name, *Caldo de Ajo* (Garlic Soup).

¼ cup olive oil   1 cup toasted breadcrumbs
2 cloves garlic   2 eggs
5 cups water   salt and pepper
pinch of saffron

Peel the garlic, bruise it slightly, and brown it carefully in hot olive oil. In the meantime, bring the water to a boil and stir in the saffron, crumbs, and well-beaten eggs. Now, remove the garlic from the oil and add the latter to the broth. Season with salt and a bit of pepper and serve at once. Serves 4.

Sopa Herbida (Boiled Soup)

This is a simple country soup, similar to *Caldo Borracho* (page 54). The boarders had only to mention it, and Angelita would exclaim, beaming: *"Delicioso!"*

4 slices bread   5 cups Angelita's Beef Stock
2 cloves garlic   (page 49) or water
2 tablespoons olive oil   salt and pepper
4 eggs

Tear or cut the bread in small pieces. Peel and mince the garlic. Heat the oil in a heavy pan that can go into the oven, and gently fry the bread and garlic. In the meantime, bring five cups of water or stock to a boil. When the bread and garlic are golden, add the salt and pepper. Allow the pan to cool slightly and then pour in the boiling water. Cook and stir for five minutes. Carefully break the eggs into the soup and place the pan in a 350° oven. Bake for approximately five or ten minutes or until the eggs are just set. Serves 4.

Sopa de Chorizo (Soup with Chorizo)

2 cups diced potatoes	1 small onion, chopped
1 cup sliced carrots (or grated)	3 tablespoons chopped parsley
	1 teaspoon salt
2 one-pound cans chick peas	pepper
4 whole cloves	1 pound *chorizo* (pages 126–128)
3 bay leaves	3 hard-cooked egg yolks

Cook potatoes and carrots in 1½ quarts boiling water about 20 minutes, or until tender. Remove vegetables from water; set aside. Simmer *chorizo* 20 minutes, drain, skin, and slice. Purée chick peas and add to water with onion, parsley, cloves, and bay leaves. Simmer 25 to 30 minutes. Remove bay leaves and cloves. Add reserved cooked vegetables and *chorizo* and heat through. Serve garnished with chopped egg yolks. Serves 6–8.

SOPA DE PESCADOS Y MARISCOS
(Fish and Shellfish Soups)

Sopa de Pescado (Fish Soup)

The quality of this soup depends on the quality and variety of fish used. In Navarre, Angelita had the delicate *merluza* and *rapé* fish to choose from, with the possible addition of small crabs and a vast assortment of shellfish. In San Francisco, she selected halibut, sea bass, or small rock fish, and sometimes added mussels or clams. In any case, the small fish are left whole (though they are cleaned, of course), and the shellfish are left in their shells.

1½ pounds fish	1 tablespoon olive oil
1 medium onion	1 teaspoon lemon juice
2 cloves garlic	salt and pepper
1 tomato	pinch of saffron
1 small bunch parsley	6 cups water

Mince the garlic and onion, quarter the tomato, and tie the parsley well. Put all the ingredients in a large pot and cover with cold water. Bring to a boil, and simmer—covered—for about 15 minutes or until the fish is just tender. Remove the fish to a warm serving plate and reserve for use as a *second course*. Strain the broth, discarding the vegetables, and serve. Sometimes Angelita added diced raw cabbage and potatoes (about one half cup each) to the strained broth, simmering it until the vegetables were tender. Serves 4–6.

Sopa de Pescado con Verduras (Fish Soup with Vegetables)

1½ pounds fish (see *Sopa de Pescado,* page 56)	2 bell peppers
	1 tomato
1 tablespoon olive oil	2 teaspoons minced parsley
1 onion	6 cups water
2 cloves garlic	salt and pepper

Mince the onion and garlic and slice the peppers. Fry them in hot olive oil until they are golden. Now add the tomato, quartered, and the parsley. Put in the fish and cover with water. Add salt and pepper to taste. Cover the pot and simmer the soup for 15 minutes, or until the fish is tender. Remove the fish to a serving platter. The soup is served with the vegetables left in. Serve the fish after the soup—as a second course. Serves 4–6.

Sopa de Almejas (Clam Soup)

2 dozen small clams	5 tablespoons minced parsley
1 tablespoon olive oil	6 cups boiling water
1 medium onion	salt and pepper
2 cloves garlic	1 cup croutons
1 tomato	

Put the clams and oil in a heavy covered skillet over medium heat and allow the clams to steam open. This will take approximately 5 minutes. Remove the clams from the pan and shell them or not, as preferred. Mince the onion and garlic and chop the tomato. Fry these, along with the parsley, in the same pan in which the clams were steamed. When the vegetables are tender, put them, with the clams and boiling water, in a soup pot. Simmer the soup for 10 minutes. Sprinkle croutons on each serving. Serves 4.

Sopa de Ostras (Oyster Soup)

Basque oyster soup is similar to American oyster stew but not half as rich. The flavor is delicate—and delicious.

2 cups shelled oysters	1½ cups water
3½ cups milk	salt and pepper

Put all the ingredients in a pan and allow to simmer gently for about 10 minutes. Just before serving add salt and pepper to taste. Serves 4.

Sopa de Gambas (Prawn Soup)

This, like the *Sopa de Bacalao* that follows, is a classic Basque soup. One must acquire a taste for both.

½ pound raw prawns	1 clove garlic
6 cups water	1 tomato
1 teaspoon salt	1 bell pepper
1 tablespoon olive oil	1 cup croutons
1 medium onion	

Rinse the prawns and cover them with six cups water. Add the salt. Bring to a boil and simmer until the prawns are pink—about 15 minutes. Remove the prawns, and drain and chill them to be used later as an appetizer or in a salad. Reserve the stock.

Chop the vegetables and fry them in olive oil until they are golden. Strain the prawn stock into the vegetables, add a pinch of pepper, and simmer five minutes. Sprinkle croutons on each serving. Serves 4–6.

Sopa de Bacalao (Codfish Soup)

Liking *Sopa de Bacalao* is, for many, an acquired taste. Angelita served it often, but there were some of her guests who never could seem to develop a great fondness for this soup. Angelita would shake her head sadly, for it was one of her favorites. But she always saw to it that anyone who turned down *Sopa de Bacalao* was served an extra-large portion of one of her other courses.

1 pound dry salt cod	⅛ teaspoon pepper
1 large clove garlic	1 teaspoon vinegar
1 tablespoon olive oil	4 slices day-old French bread
¼ cup breadcrumbs	

Freshen the cod by allowing it to soak overnight in water to cover. Change the water several times. Drain well, cover with fresh water, and bring just to a boil. Drain and reserve the cod until ready to use.

To make the soup, simmer the codfish in one piece in 8 cups water.

(Do not allow it to boil.) In the meantime, mash the garlic, bread-crumbs, oil, vinegar, and pepper in a mortar. When the fish flakes easily (about 15 minutes) remove it to a warm serving platter to be served as a separate course. Stir the garlic-crumb paste into the broth and simmer for ten minutes. Taste for seasoning. Top each serving with a slice of French bread. Serves 4–6.

Sopa de Anguilas (*Eel Soup*)

Sopa de Anguilas is a very old and very popular Basque dish. The Biscay coast and the many streams that tumble into it from the Pyrenees abound in eels. And—unlike many American fisherman who fling a hooked eel back into the water—the Basque is highly pleased to bring home this slithery catch.

2 or 3 eels (1-1½ pounds each)	¼ teaspoon pepper
¼ cup olive oil	1 tablespoon flour
1 medium onion	8 cups boiling water
1 clove garlic	¼ cup dry white wine
1 bunch leeks	1 bay leaf
2 teaspoons salt	2 tablespoons parsley

Clean the eels, skin them, and remove their heads and tails. Cut the meat in small pieces and rinse in fresh water. Pat the meat dry with a paper towel. Peel and mince the onion and garlic, and cut the leeks in thin slices. Fry the vegetables in oil until they are just tender. Now add the eel, stirring so that it will not stick. When the eel is just beginning to become golden, stir in the flour, salt, and pepper. Now add the other ingredients; allow to come to a boil, lower the heat, and simmer gently for 30 minutes, or until the eel is tender. Skim off any excess fat. Remove the bay leaf before serving. Serves 6.

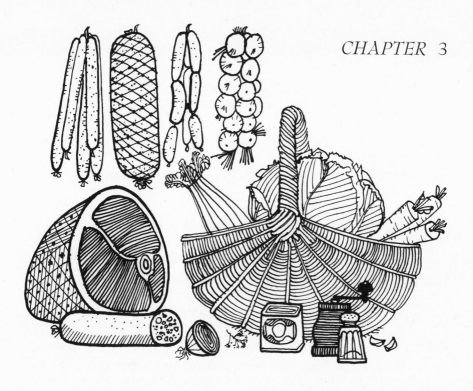

CHAPTER 3

La Vaporina

Asko dakik bizitxen baldin ba dakik.
Mucho sabes si sabes vivir.
You know much if you know how to live.

It was May 9, 1911—the day after Angelita and Martin were married. In the soft pre-sunrise gray, Angelita awoke. And, like her, the city was also awakening. Through the window—its usually crisp-starched curtains now hanging limp from the night's fog—the rattle of trucks from the Produce Market, the creak of rope and chain as the

61

ships along the Embarcadero pulled at their moorings, the scream of seagulls haggling over ownership of a fish, or perhaps some bread and meat scraps tossed overboard by a galley boy.

Close beside her, Martin slept on, unaware of the coming of day. But when Angelita reached out, shyly, to put her hand into that of her new husband's, his responding clasp—even in his sleep—was immediately and totally aware.

A warm, happy, overwhelming feeling swept through her. She would have liked to stay right where she was forever. But, no. Sliding softly out of bed, she made ready for the day.

La Vaporina was still asleep when Angelita came downstairs, though it would not be for long. In the six weeks she had been in San Francisco, and helping in the hotel's kitchen, she had begun to know the way of the boarders. Most of them had become accustomed to the eggs and meat of a typical American breakfast. But cooking these could always be postponed for a time. Not so, the traditional Basque-type breakfast. As soon as the men were dressed and downstairs they must have their *café con leche,* slabs of bread, and the inevitable glass of whisky.

Angelita hurried through the small dining room where the oil-cloth-topped table was already set with thick white plates and sturdy silverware, dully glowing in the gray dawn. She switched on the light in the kitchen, quickly filled the coffeepot and set it on one of the gas burners. Two kettles of milk went on the stove, too. One for *café con leche* for Martin and the boarders, the other for chocolate for herself and Ramona, who would now be working as Angelita's assistant.

Now the bread. Angelita unbolted the back door and stepped out into the cement patio. At her feet sat the baker's cloth-covered basket, its wicker sides still warm, for the several dozen loaves within were only minutes out of the oven.

A continuing surprise—that the bread would arrive in such a manner. The contrast to Pamplona, where she had cooked for the Aldabe family who had owned over half her own little village (Gorriz), brought a wistful smile. In Pamplona, fresh baker's bread had meant a ten-minute walk through musty streets, so narrow that the sun warmed them only at midday. Then there was the wait in line before the high window of the *panadería* and the gossip with friends. The window would at last slide open, the line begin to move, as loaf after hot golden loaf passed into the string bags of the waiting buyers.

In San Francisco, Angelita, shaking her head a little sadly, picked up the bread basket at her door. Above, fog shreds made pink by the rising sun, swirled gently against the blue sky. She breathed in the early morning crispness, a saltwater-tar tang with, sometimes, overtones of roasting coffee and baking bread. A heady combination of odors that she was coming to find peculiarly and forever San Francisco. Another deep breath and she turned back to the kitchen.

Coffee to measure, chocolate to grate, bread to slice. A sound at the dining-room door. Martin! At once bashful and strong, his arms were about her momentarily, his mouth pressed against her hair. "Good morning, Angelita mine." A long look into each others' eyes, and then, at the scrubbed pine table next to the stove, they sat down to their first breakfast as man and wife.

For Angelita, most of the day that followed was typical of those to come. Martin had barely finished his *café con leche* and crusty bread when the first boarders thumped downstairs. Most of them made right for the stove and poured their own coffee and hot milk. Then they converged around the dining-room table or took their cups—and an overflowing platter of bread—into the bar, where Martin had gone to pour the little glasses of morning whisky.

Angelita could hear the muffled voices and the lusty laughter she knew meant the telling of traditional Basque and Galacian jokes intended solely for the benefit of a new groom. She smiled at the teasing, though her ears did become faintly red at thought of the stories.

Martin must bear his own discomfort. After all, it was the expected thing. She, on the other hand, had her work to do. The men would be

63

finishing their coffee and bread, and the whisky would have given them new appetites.

Most of the boarders were seamen on shore between voyages. But six had jobs in the city and so their breakfasts must be on time. The others would eat at their leisure, some of the very late risers breakfasting only an hour or so before the first sitting for lunch.

There were eggs to beat for omlets, ham to cut and fry, as well as potatoes and onions to slice for *tortilla de patatas.*

Too, there was the soup stock to set simmering, and the dinner roast to take from the icebox so it would be at the right room temperature for seasoning before it went into the oven.

There was constant coming and going in the kitchen now. Martin appeared briefly to check the vegetable supplies in the icebox and in the little shed just outside the back door. Then, with a soft farewell to Angelita, he was off to the Produce Market and, later, to Fisherman's Wharf.

The door opened again, and it was Ramona. *"Buenos dias. Muy buenos dias."* And she was out of her coat and into her apron almost before there was time to acknowledge the greeting.

"Buenos dias, Angelita." It was Juanita, Ramona's sister, popping her head in the kitchen briefly before she hurried upstairs to straighten the rooms.

All morning the boarders came and went. They were, happily, never all in the kitchen at once, and they were never under foot. Angelita found the constant traffic mildly disconcerting. But Ramona, who knew the ways of La Vaporina, was reassuring: "Ah, they have teased Martin with one naughty story or another, you can be sure. Now, like puppies or bad little boys, they come to wish the bride well, so that she will know they have gentlemanly manners and meant no offense to the groom."

❅ ❅

Summer came to San Francisco, and a strange sort of summer indeed, Angelita thought. The once bright skies of spring were, for days, gray with fog. Sometimes the Bay—though merely two blocks away—was invisible, the only suggestion of activity on its waters evidenced by the cacophony of fog horns and bell buoys or the lonely, questioning wail of ships' horns as vessels moved hesitantly toward moorings or open water.

It was during that summer that Martin decided to remodel La Vaporina. His plans for enlarging the ground floor were not new; Angelita had been in San Francisco scarcely a day before Martin had proudly outlined his ideas.

However, on the evening he announced, "On Monday, the carpenters come to start the new kitchen," Angelita could not help but feel that something dear and familiar—though briefly known—was about to be taken away. Nevertheless, as Martin pointed out, it was a good time to remodel. Most of the regular boarders, the Galacians, were out to sea, and—because it was the busy season in the mines and lumber camps—there should be few casual guests.

So Monday came and so did the carpenters, along with trucks of lumber, barrels of nails, rolls of roofing paper, and vast assortments of hammers, saws, and chisels.

There followed a full month of daily upheaval and sawdust. Where there had been open patio there was now a roof. What had once been the inside kitchen wall became space—the center of the new dining room. Wall became door. Door became window. And through it all, Angelita prepared three meals a day, Martin attended to all the business details and officiated at the bar—and the several boarders in residence and the outsiders who dropped in for lunch or dinner were made as comfortably unaware, as possible, of La Vaporina's major overhaul.

When the last carpenter had picked up his tools, when the last shred of sawdust had been wiped away, Angelita and Martin surveyed their new surroundings.

The new dining room, freshly plastered and whitewashed, now had two long wood tables plus a small square one, and enough chairs and benches to seat at least thirty people at one time. The old wood floor, worn smooth by the tramping of feet and the daily wet-mopping, now was covered with shiny linoleum.

But it was the kitchen that Angelita liked best. The remodeling had not altered its familiarity, after all. And as she stood in the doorway, her hand in Martin's, there was a fleeting guilt for her earlier doubts about the changes.

There was the same old six-burner gas stove with its oven so big that four legs of lamb could be roasted in it at once, with even some space left over. Next to it was a new addition—a mammoth wood and coal stove. Angelita, recalling the temperamental wood stoves in Gorriz and Pamplona, had mixed feelings about this.

"A wood stove is like a burro," she had chided Martin when he told her of the purchase. "It has its own mind and will stop or get going when it wants, no matter how it is teased or prodded."

"Yes," Martin's blue eyes twinkled, "and, like a burro, it is steady and strong, and a good friend for life."

Above the stoves and behind the work areas on either side of the deep double sink hung utensils in lavish array. Gleaming steel frying pans ranging from one-omelet size to a grand and unwieldly skillet that would hold a dozen chops all at the same time. There were saucepans, some with metal handles so that they could go into the oven; sauté pans with their deep straight sides; stew kettles in graduated sizes like an army of overgrown measuring cups.

Arranged at intervals were stirring spoons and ladles, wire whisks and basting brushes, colanders and sieves. Low open shelves held roasting pans and baking sheets, a squad of casseroles, and a nest of earthenware mixing bowls. There were a pepper mill, scales, a mortar and pestle, and gleaming steel kitchen knives in all sizes.

66

One wall was all white: white icebox flanked by white-painted shelves stacked high with heavy white china plates, cups, and bowls.

Last, there was the corner Angelita liked best. And, wonderfully, in its move it had not lost its homeliness. That spot opposite the sink and close to the stoves that held the sturdy wooden table and bench. It was at this table, its top smoothed by constant scrubbing, that Martin and Angelita had their breakfast each morning—a scant time alone together before the boarders awoke or the outside help arrived.

Here Angelita would sit to clean or pare vegetables. And sometimes, on long mornings, a boarder—homesick for the rolling hills of Navarre or the pounding surf of Galacia—would sit with her and exchange stories of the past.

And it was inevitable that, sooner or later, he would ask, "Can I help you, Angelita? A *cocido* tonight? A carrot to scrape? An onion to peel? My eyes are so burned by the heat of the sun, the salt of the sea, that even an onion brings not one tear. Let me help you."

Cocidos (Boiled Dinners)

Cocidos (*cocido* means "boiled") are popular one-dish meals, probably of peasant origin. They are combinations of meats, poultry, vegetables, and beans—whatever is readily available. But they all have one thing in common: the use of at least one piece of smoked meat.

Sometimes the *cocido* is served, everything at once, in large soup bowls. At other times the broth is strained and served, with vermicelli or rice in it, as a first course, and the meat is sliced and arranged, with the vegetables, on a platter for the second course.

Cocido I

1 pound lean beef stew meat	1 medium onion
½ chicken	1 clove garlic
¼ pound salt pork	1 carrot
1 small ham bone or ham hock	2 stalks celery
	4 medium potatoes
½ pound *chorizo* (pages 126–128)	1 cup dried *garbanzos**
1 small cabbage	salt and pepper

Cut up the vegetables. Put all the ingredients except the *chorizo* and potatoes in a large soup kettle. Cover with cold water, bring to a boil, and reduce heat. Cover and simmer for approximately 2 hours. Put the *chorizo,* with water to cover, in a separate pan and simmer for 15 minutes. Drain well to remove excess fat. Then add the *chorizo* to the *Cocido.* The potatoes are added to the pot during the last half-hour of cooking. Serves 6.

* If dried *garbanzos* are used, they must first be soaked overnight in warm water with a teaspoon of salt. Two or three cups of canned *garbanzos* may be substituted for one cup of dried. Drain them and add at the same time as the potatoes.

Cocido II

3 beef shortribs, sawed in half	1 onion
1 small ham bone or ham hock	1 clove garlic
	2 leeks
1 stewing chicken	1 cup *garbanzos*
2 turnips	4 medium potatoes
1 cabbage	salt and pepper

Cut the chicken in serving-size pieces. Then proceed as for *Cocido I* (above). Serves 6.

Cocido III

3 beef shortribs, sawed in half
½ blood sausage
6 links *chorizo* (pages 126–128)
¼ pound salt pork
1 cup *garbanzos*

2 cloves garlic
pinch of saffron
4 medium potatoes
salt and pepper

Put all the ingredients except the blood sausage, *chorizo,* and potatoes in a large soup kettle. Add water to cover, and proceed as for *Cocido I* (page 68). Add the blood sausage and the *chorizo* for the last hour-and-a-half of cooking time. Serves 6.

Cocido IV

1 2-pound stewing hen
2-pound ham shank
1 cup dry *garbanzos*
1 cup dry navy beans
2 cloves garlic
pinch saffron

4 large potatoes
1 head white cabbage
¼ cup rice
¼ cup vermicelli
salt and pepper

Soak the *garbanzos* overnight in lukewarm water with a teaspoon of salt. Drain and tie loosely in a cheesecloth bag. Tie the navy beans in another cheesecloth bag. (Be sure that both bags are loose enough so that the *garbanzos* and beans have room to swell.) Tie the legs and wings of the hen so that they will stay in place.

Put the hen, ham, *garbanzos,* and beans in a large pot. Cover with cold water. Add the garlic, minced, and a pinch of saffron. Cover the pot, bring to a boil, skim any foam. Lower heat and simmer, covered, for 1½ hours. Remove the navy beans.

Dice the cabbage, parboil, and drain. Add it to the pot along with

69

the diced potatoes, rice, and vermicelli broken in small pieces. Cover and simmer for 20 minutes or until the rice is tender.

Remove the chicken, ham, and *garbanzos*. Slice the meats and arrange on a serving platter with the beans at one end, the *garbanzos* at the other. Season the broth with salt and pepper to taste and serve it as the first course. Serves 8.

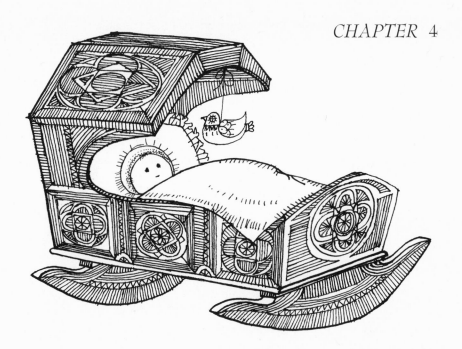

CHAPTER 4

Marty is Born

Bat izatea obe, bi itxo egitea bano.
Es mejor tener uno, que esperar dos.
It is better to have one, than expect two.

The year passed, and it was a morning in June, 1912. The breakfast coffee and chocolate were hot, the bread was sliced, and the bacon and eggs were ready to be dropped into a skillet. Angelita filled the stock pot at the sink, but when she went to lift it to the stove, it was as though riveted where it sat. Sighing, she emptied the pot so that it could be moved, and filled it at the stove with endless dipperfuls of water

71

carried one by one. She dropped in the short ribs, the garlic, onion, carrots, and celery. A shake of salt. The lid rattled tremulously as she put it in place.

She took off her apron, folded it neatly, and went into the bar where Martin was already at work.

"It is time."

Martin, his face suddenly pale, helped her upstairs and hurried right back down. Phone calls to make.

"Juanita, *buenos dias.* You can help Ramona in the kitchen today? It is Angelita's time."

"You can come to be with my Angelita, Doña Maria? It is her time. *Gracias, muchas gracias.*"

During the succeeding hours, Martin polished every glass and bottle behind the bar. Then he went outside and hosed down the front of La Vaporina, though it had only had its regular weekly scrubbing three days before. Back inside, he lined up each bar stool at perfect angles. Then he rearranged the already neatly stacked glasses and bar equipment.

Those boarders who did not have regular jobs lingered at the tables opposite the bar, thumbing through newspapers or making stilted conversation, or glancing at the clock whose hands seemed never to move.

A lusty squall echoed from upstairs. Or did it? Were the men so tense that their ears were playing tricks? Another squall—and then another and another. No. It was true. The baby had come!

All the men looked at Martin, and he—hands clenched on the bar —looked at the stairs. A door opening, quick footsteps in the upstairs hall, and Doña Maria's face appeared at the landing.

"Martin. Martin. Come now. You are a papá! A boy, Martin!"

The rest of the day was running upstairs to look at the baby or hold Angelita's hand gently in his, and running downstairs to pour drinks for the men and receive their congratulations. Then upstairs again. How tiny was his new son. Martin's blue eyes became soft.

Next morning the first boarders tiptoed self-consciously downstairs. Most were bachelors and unsure how to act with a new baby in the house. They pushed open the kitchen door and there, in her accustomed place at the scrubbed pine table, slicing bread and piling it on plates, was Angelita.

Sheepishly, for they wondered if their celebration of the previous day had not disturbed her, the men lined up one by one to extend their blessings. *"Buenos dias,* Mamá—*Muy buenos dias,* Mamá—God bless you, little Mamá—" It was a new name, falling naturally from their tongues. And seldom again would any of the boarders, or the many patrons to come, ever call Angelita anything else but *"Mamá."*

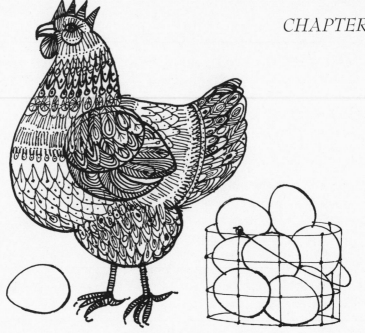

CHAPTER 5

The New Hotel

Aberast izatea bano izen ona obeago.
Mejor buena fama, que ser rico.
Better a good name than riches.

La Vaporina—the little ship—had at last become too small. In the six years of their life together, Papá (Martin, too, had gained a new name) and Mamá had worked hard—to be rewarded with an increasing number of guests and more work.

So, now, standing behind the bar—a forgotten glass of whisky in his hand—Papá's mind was alive with problems and plans for the future, which each day came closer.

There was, he realized, no possible way to expand La Vaporina. The brick walls could not be pushed out. And, sturdy as they were, they would not safely support a third story. So, then, what to do with the potential boarders, more arriving all the time? What to say to the would-be diners, who hearing of Mamá's cooking through a friend, or the friend of a friend, hopefully pushed open the front door each evening?

Mamá was well aware of Papá's thoughts, though he did not discuss them with her. For woman's work was to manage the kitchen; keep an eye on their two little boys, Marty—now nearly five—and the baby, Luis, who was just learning to toddle; and supervise her two younger sisters, Antonia and Paca, who had arrived from Spain in 1914.

But a man who liked to be doing something could not forever keep his thoughts within himself. So, on early afternoons, when the bar was usually deserted, Papá would walk a few doors up Broadway to his friend, the tavern owner Santiago Aranguren.

"Yes, yes. It is true: La Vaporina is now too small."

"And the tavern. Not too small, perhaps, but, as you say, the waterfront is changing. The strikes now. And the sailors. They are not the same as in the old days—"

"A rougher lot, no? Not steady. Too much drinking. A whisky to whet the appetite is good. A man needs this. But too much whisky. It sours the stomach—and my patience."

"But Broadway is a good street. You would not leave it?"

"Leave Broadway? No. Never. Broadway is the greatest street in the City. But it is *up* Broadway that the best business will be. This I feel. I am very sure."

And so the conversation went. In no time talking turned into doing, and either Papá or Santiago would be walking up and down Broadway, looking for a chance empty building or "For Sale" sign, following up any tips that someone along the street might be considering selling.

75

For, without benefit of documents or legal seals, Papá and Santiago—in the tradition that becomes a Basque—had become partners.

So it was that, early in 1917, they heard of a sheepherders' hotel whose owner wanted to retire.

The hotel was on Broadway. And, as if that were not enough, it was located barely a block from where Broadway was so *"up"* (a sheer rock cliff, in fact) that the street was forced to end there. This was the same cliff that Papá had leaned against on his first afternoon in San Francisco—when, looking down the full length of Broadway—he had made the decision to become a hotel man.

The months between the finding of the new hotel and the actual moving were hectic. First, buyers must be found for La Vaporina and for Santiago's tavern.

Next, the new hotel must have a name. *La Vaporina,* again? A fine name for the little hotel on the Embarcadero, but—no—not suitable for a hotel at the top of Broadway. *Basque Hotel?* But again, no. That name already had been taken by someone else. Then, what about *Hotel Español?* Appropriate. (Papá and Santiago had both come from the north of Spain.) *Hotel Español*—it had a nice sound to it, too. Papá immediately hired a man to paint the sign.

Then, there was a new bar to buy. Not that the hotel lacked a bar —but simply that the one it did have was in such disrepair. One look at its nicks and scratches, alcohol rings and cigarette burns, and Papá, shaking his head, set out for the used furniture shops on McAllister Street.

The search lasted several days and nearly didn't end when it did. For the bar Papá at last selected was one he almost passed up. And no wonder! The solid dark mahogany of the bar and its intricately hand-carved back-bar, the brass inlaid hand-rest and even the solid brass foot-rail were entirely (yes, every inch) masked with layers of bilious green enamel.

How much scraping and rubbing there must be to return it to its original magnificence! Making out a check and arranging for delivery, Papá wondered at man's wantonness.

Finally there was the decorating. Papá and Santiago worked long hours carefully planning what would go where and which color paint would look best. They measured windows for curtains, and pondered a full day in the yard goods sections of The White House and The City of Paris department stores before they decided upon their purchases. And Papá found a series of paintings of fruits and flowers—each nicely framed—to hang in a neat row on the second floor landing of Hotel Español.

And, as in the initial decision to buy a new hotel, Mamá was not consulted. For this, too, was man's work.

However, no sooner was the paint dry and the new furniture installed at Hotel Español than Papá hurried into La Vaporina's kitchen —careful not to upset young Marty who had built himself a potato and onion fortress behind the swinging door, or awaken infant son Luis who was dozing in his high chair near the scrubbed pine table.

"Come, Angelita." Gently impatient now, his fingers untied her apron, "Come see how nicely our new home is prepared. Walk with me to the Español. Antonia or Paca can watch the boys. And the soup, too. Come. Now."

It was a beautiful day for an outing, even Mamá had to admit. And it really was an outing for her who chose to spend almost all her time— except for morning Mass—inside La Vaporina, and particularly its warm and fragrant kitchen.

Walking up Broadway, crossing wide Columbus Avenue with Italian names on every store front, glimpsing a bit of curious Chinatown, Mamá was reminded of six years before, when she and Segundo had come this very way. How frightened she had been that day. How strange and foreign the new sights—the smells. And the stab of regret and homesickness for having ever left Navarre—a feeling that she'd not dare admit, even to herself.

77

How different now! Mamá breathed in the October air with its San Francisco salt-tar-roasting-coffee-baking-bread tang. Yes, how different, how warm and full life was. The firm hand under her elbow: a part of her very self. She looked up at Papá and he, catching her long glance, thought that she had never looked more beautiful and wondered at the benefits of a walk in the fresh air.

They were in front of Hotel Español. It was sandwiched snugly between two buildings, one proclaiming itself "The Parisian French Bakery," the other, "Figeac Bros.—Groceries." While Papá tried his key in the new lock, Mamá looked above her at the freshly painted sign and the rows of polished, starched-curtained windows on the second and third floors. *Twenty-two* rooms upstairs! She could hardly imagine.

The door swung open, and taking Mamá's hand in his—exactly as on the day he had first shown her La Vaporina and on the day they had walked together through remodeled La Vaporina—Papá began the tour.

The street door opened right into the bar-room. There, filling all one side wall, was Papá's magnificent bar. The brass inlays and foot rail were polished so they glistened like pure gold. The fine wood, relieved of its enamel coating, had a warm glow. Papá ran his hand proudly along its smooth surface as he led Mamá toward the dining room.

At the far end of the bar, was a little glass-enclosed office with a roll-top desk. Papá had already sat at the desk, looked through the polished glass, seen the many guests to come, heard the future songs, laughter, and conversation. Sitting there alone in the empty room, a feeling of self-pride—even vanity—had allowed itself to slip in. But for only an instant.

Today, still ashamed of that momentary preening, Papá hurried Mamá past the office a little brusquely.

The dining room—especially if one compared it with La Vaporina —was not only big but bright. The white oilcloth on the two tables, running the full length of the room, reflected the pressed-tin ceiling with its delicate floral pattern outlined in off-white. The blankness of the soft green walls was relieved by pictures of the Basque country that Papá and Santiago had tacked up at methodically regular intervals.

How many chairs! Mamá's mind immediately began computing bowls of soup, platters of beans, and slices of roast lamb. And from the future her mind jumped to the present.

"It is late, Martin. We must go. The roast—Antonia might forget to baste it often enough. And the *omelets*—I must make those myself."

Papá sighed. Being a man, and the oldest Abaurrea in California (Uncle Cleto having returned to Spain the very year Martin came to San Francisco), Papá was now the patriarch. He was the decision-maker and guardian of a growing family: his wife, his two little sons, his wife's two young sisters, and his own niece—all in San Francisco; and—in Hollister—two of Mamá's brothers and two of Papá's nephews.

Yet, even as patriarch, he knew that it was not his right to interfere with a well-run kitchen. What was the first phrase the Devil had spoken after seven years of trying to learn to speak Basque? *"Bai, Anderra."* ("Yes, Ma'am.") Perhaps the Devil had a good reason.

Mamá must get back to make the omelets. So the rest of the tour of Hotel Español must wait.

Huevos (*Eggs*)

Every market in the Basque provinces has at least one stall where eggs are sold. The choicest are packed, by sixes, in clear plastic cartons, and displayed prominently. The other eggs, graded by size and freshness, are piled in deep bins, and there is always a selection of cracked eggs at reduced prices.

The shopper can buy one egg or a basketful. Usually it is the latter, for, although eggs are seldom served for breakfast, they make their daily appearance as a separate course for dinner or supper. And they play a big part in desserts.

We mentioned this difference in egg-eating habits to our hostess during a visit to Navarre. And the next morning there was a surprise for us: an American-style breakfast of bacon and eggs, toast and jam, and black coffee. Surprise indeed! For our American breakfast was preceded by the usual Basque breakfast: rolls, sliced *chorizo* and *salchichón, churros,* and great cups of thick hot chocolate.

Just as there is always a squat basket of eggs in every kitchen in the Basque country, there was always a shelf reserved for eggs in La Vaporina's icebox. Mamá discovered that she was cooking a tremendous number of eggs. For many of the boarders liked the American idea of eggs for breakfast but, at the same time, they could not forego the Basque custom of an egg course for dinner and/or supper, too.

Huevos Revueltos con Calabaza (*Eggs Scrambled with Zucchini*)

1 tablespoon olive oil	1 cup leftover cooked zucchini
½ medium onion	8 eggs
½ clove garlic	salt and pepper
1 small tomato	

Mince the onion and garlic and fry them gently in olive oil until the vegetables are golden. Seed and dice the tomato and add it to the pan, along with the zucchini. Allow to heat through. Now pour in the well-beaten eggs, seasoned with a little salt and pepper. Stir and cook gently until the eggs are set. Serves 4.

80

Huevos Revueltos con Pimientos
(*Eggs Scrambled with Peppers*)

1 tablespoon olive oil	1 clove garlic
2 bell peppers or one 7-ounce can pimientos	8 eggs
1 medium onion	salt and pepper

Mince the peppers, onion, and garlic, and fry them gently in olive oil until the vegetables are limp. Beat the eggs well with a little salt and pepper and pour over the vegetables. Cook slowly, stirring several times, until the eggs are set. Serves 4.

TORTILLAS (*Omelets*)

Basque omelets, when perfectly made, are firm enough to stand proudly on a serving plate. Yet they are, at the same time, tender and light. Some practice is therefore necessary—but, first of all, the correct pan.

Mamá preferred a cast iron skillet with two-inch sloping sides: a six-inch pan for a four-egg omelet and a nine-inch pan for eight eggs. She first treated a new pan by scrubbing it well with steel wool and cleansing powder. Then it was rinsed, dried, and heated for a minute or two. Now a little olive oil was rubbed all over the inside of the pan and it was allowed to stand overnight. Before Mamá used the pan for its first omelet, she heated it again and rubbed it well with a paper towel.

Her omelet pans were never used for anything else—this insured that they would remain "stick-free." Also, they were never washed, but merely wiped clean with a paper towel, then rubbed lightly with oil and put away for the next time.

As to the making of omelets themselves, here are Mamá's rules: Be sure that the sides of the pan as well as the bottom are oiled; use medium heat; beat the eggs well; and, as the omelet is cooking, keep lifting along the edges with a spatula to keep the edges free and high and to give the uncooked part a chance at direct heat. When the omelet is nearly firm, invert it quickly. It is possible to use a spatula for this. An easier method, however, is to cover the pan with a small plate and invert both, dropping the omelet onto the plate. Then slip the omelet back into the pan, browned side up. Let the second side brown and serve immediately.

Tortilla de Jamón (Ham Omelet)

> olive oil
> ¼ pound ham
> 8 eggs
> salt and pepper

Dice the ham and brown it in a little oil. Season with salt and pepper. Add the well-beaten eggs and follow the *Tortilla* directions above. Serves 4.

Tortilla de Chorizo (Chorizo Omelet)

> 3 links *chorizo* (pages 126–128)
> 8 eggs

Peel and slice the *chorizo* and fry (no oil is necessary) for 10 minutes. Drain excess fat. Add the well-beaten eggs and proceed as for *Tortillas* (above). Serves 4.

Tortilla de Patatas (Potato Omelet)

Over the centuries, *Tortilla de Patatas* has been a staple of Basque family meals, both urban and country. Any of this *tortilla* that's left over is excellent for a snack. Invariably, one finds platters of it, cut in wedges and stuck with toothpicks, arranged along the bars of the Basque provinces. And there is never a Basque picnic without it: usually served sandwich-fashion in a split loaf of French bread.

1 tablespoon olive oil
3 medium potatoes
1 thin slice of onion (optional)
8 eggs
salt and pepper

Peel and slice the potatoes and chop the onion. Fry slowly in olive oil, shaking the pan and stirring, until the potatoes are tender and slightly golden. Season with salt and pepper. Pour in the well-beaten eggs, and proceed as for *Tortillas* (page 82). Serves 4.

Tortilla de Berenjena (Eggplant Omelet)

2 tablespoons olive oil
1 medium-sized eggplant
8 eggs
salt and pepper

Peel the eggplant and dice it into small cubes. Fry it gently in olive oil until the eggplant is tender, but do not allow it to brown. Season with salt and pepper, pour in the well-beaten eggs, and proceed as for *Tortillas* (page 82). Serves 4.

83

Tortilla de Setas (*Mushroom Omelet*)

After the first spring rains and on through early summer, mushrooms dot the meadows of the Basque provinces. So Mamá, like most Basques, learned to tell edible mushrooms from dangerous ones as soon as she learned to walk.

Fresh mushrooms are, of course, best for omelets. But if they are unavailable in meadow or store, canned ones can be substituted.

1 tablespoon olive oil	8 eggs
1 clove garlic	1 tablespoon minced parsley
1 cup sliced mushrooms	salt and pepper

Mince the garlic and fry it slowly in olive oil. When the garlic is just beginning to brown, add the mushrooms along with a little salt and pepper. Stir and cook for three or four minutes. Now add the eggs that have been beaten well with the parsley. Proceed as for *Tortillas* (page 82). Serves 4.

Tortilla de Pimientos (*Pimiento Omelet*)

This is a highly popular Basque dish, both because of its excellent flavor and its colorful likeness to the red and green of the Basque flag.

Use two fresh bell peppers, one green and one red. Or use one green pepper and two canned pimientos. Or, if no fresh peppers are available, use one seven-ounce can of pimientos and one tablespoon minced parsley. Do, in any case, adhere to the red and green color combination.

1 tablespoon olive oil	1 small clove garlic
2 bell peppers (or alternates above)	8 eggs
1 small onion	salt and pepper

84

Chop the vegetables well and fry gently in olive oil, shaking the pan from time to time, until the vegetables are tender. Season with salt and pepper, and pour in the well-beaten eggs. Stir, and proceed as for *Tortillas* (page 82). Serves 4.

Tortilla de Esparragos (*Asparagus Omelet*)

1 tablespoon olive oil
8 or 12 stalks cooked or
 canned asparagus
8 eggs
salt and pepper

Cut the asparagus spears in one-inch pieces and fry gently in olive oil for five minutes. Shake the pan often. Season with salt and pepper. Pour in the well-beaten eggs and follow the directions for *Tortillas* (page 82). Serves 4.

Tortilla de Alubias Blancas (*Navy Bean Omelet*)

1 tablespoon olive oil
½ medium onion
1 clove garlic
1 cup cooked, drained navy
 beans

1 tablespoon minced parsley
8 eggs
salt and pepper

Mince the onion and garlic and fry them in olive oil until they are tender. Stir in the navy beans, along with a little salt and pepper and the parsley. Stir and fry until the beans are heated through. Pour in the well-beaten eggs and proceed as for *Tortillas* (page 82). Serves 4.

85

Tortilla de Sardinas (Sardine Omelet)

Basques love fish, so it is not surprising that they combine one of their favorites, the sardine, with eggs. This makes an excellent late supper served with French bread and a green salad.

1 teaspoon olive oil
2 4½-ounce cans sardines
8 eggs
salt and pepper

Drain the sardines and break them into small pieces. Fry them in olive oil with a little salt and pepper. When the sardines are bubbling vigorously, add the beaten eggs and proceed as for *Tortillas* (page 82). Serves 4.

HUEVOS COCIDOS AL HORNO
(Baked Eggs)

Huevos Zarauz (Eggs, Zarauz-Style)

Zarauz is a popular little resort on the northern Cantabrian coast. This dish, that bears its name, is a perfect answer for a brunch or late supper.

For each serving allow:

1 teaspoon olive oil
½ cup cooked peas or green beans·
2 spears cooked asparagus
1 canned pimiento

2 slices *chorizo* (pages 126–128)
1 tablespoon tomato sauce
2 eggs
salt and pepper

Rub an individual baking dish with oil and arrange the peas, aspara-gus, pimiento, and *chorizo* neatly. Break the eggs into the dish and pour the tomato sauce around them. Bake in a 375° oven for 8 to 10 min-utes, or until the egg whites are set.

Jamón y Huevos (Ham and Eggs)

olive oil
4 slices baked or boiled ham
8 eggs
salt and pepper

Fry the ham in a little olive oil and place the slices in a shallow casse-role or four individual casseroles. Carefully break the eggs over the ham, season with a little salt and pepper, and bake in a 375° oven for 8 or 10 minutes, or until the egg whites are set. Serves 4.

Huevos en Salsa de Tomate (Eggs Baked in Tomato Sauce)

1 tablespoon olive oil
1 medium onion
1 clove garlic
1 bell pepper or 2 canned
   pimientos
1 #303 can solid pack
   tomatoes
1 teaspoon salt
⅛ teaspoon pepper
8 eggs

Mince the onion, garlic, and pepper, and fry them in olive oil until they are almost tender. Mash the tomatoes, and add them, along with the salt and pepper. Simmer, uncovered, until the tomatoes begin to thicken, and then pour the sauce into a shallow casserole or four individual casseroles. Break the eggs carefully into the sauce. Bake in a 375° oven for 8 to 10 minutes, or until the eggs are set. Serves 4.

Huevos con Chorizo y Verduras
(Eggs Baked with Chorizo and Vegetables)

1 tablespoon olive oil
2 cups chopped raw vegetables
  (spinach, cabbage, potatoes,
  or carrots)

1 clove garlic
4 links *chorizo* (pages 126–128)
8 eggs
salt and pepper

Chop the vegetables and mince the garlic. Cook them in the olive oil until they are just tender. Season with salt and pepper. In the meantime, peel and fry the *chorizo* for 5 minutes. Now place the vegetables in a lightly oiled casserole or four individual casseroles. Arrange the *chorizo* over them. Carefully top the dish with the raw eggs. Bake in a 375° oven for 8 to 10 minutes, or until the eggs are set. Serves 4.

Patatas con Huevos (Potatoes with Eggs)

2 tablespoons olive oil
4 medium potatoes
1 clove garlic

1 tablespoon minced parsley
8 eggs
salt and pepper

Peel the potatoes and cut them in thick rounds. Heat the oil in a casserole or skillet, add the potatoes, and cook them—turning the slices and shaking the pan—for about 15 minutes, or until the potatoes are half-cooked. Sprinkle with salt and pepper and the minced clove of garlic. Pour in just enough boiling water to barely cover the potatoes. Stir, cover, and simmer until the potatoes are done and the water has almost evaporated. Sprinkle the potatoes with minced parsley and break the eggs around the edge of the casserole. Cover and cook over low heat until the eggs are set. Or, the dish may be placed, uncovered, in a 375° oven until the eggs are done. Serves 4.

HUEVOS COCIDOS (Hardboiled Eggs)

Hardboiled eggs are usually served by the Basques as an appetizer (page 38), but they sometimes make their appearance as a lunch or supper dish—especially during Lent.

Huevos en Salsa de Codorniz (Eggs in Quail Sauce)

    8 hardboiled eggs
    1½ cups *Salsa de Codorniz*
       (page 189)
    1 tablespoon minced parsley

Shell the eggs and cut them in half, lengthwise. Place them in hot *Salsa de Codorniz,* cover, and simmer gently until the eggs are heated through. Sprinkle a little minced parsley on each serving. Serves 4.

HUEVOS REVUELTOS (Scrambled Eggs)

Piperade

Piperade is often called the Basque omelet, but it is more scrambled eggs than omelet. A memorable combination of vegetables and eggs that many like to think of as the Basque national dish. There are, consequently, many versions. But this one is Mamá's own.

Piperade

3 tablespoons bacon fat or
olive oil
1 small clove garlic
2 bell peppers
1 medium onion
1 cup drained solid pack
tomatoes or 3 fresh tomatoes
2 canned pimientos
8 eggs
½ teaspoon salt
pepper to taste

Chop the garlic, peppers, and onion well and fry them in a skillet in
the bacon fat or oil until the vegetables are transparent. Mash the tomatoes (if fresh tomatoes are used, peel, seed, and dice them) and add
them, along with the sliced pimiento, to the skillet. Cover and cook
gently for 10 or 15 minutes. Beat the eggs well and stir them carefully
into the vegetable mixture. Stir and cook until the eggs begin to set.
Overcooking will cause the dish to "weep." Serves 4.

CHAPTER 6

Moving Day

Jakiteko artzen ikasi zazu ematen.
Para aprender a recibir, aprende a dar.
To learn to receive, first learn to give.

Moving day came. Except for several of the Galacian sailors who felt they must remain near the Embarcadero, the boarders had packed their belongings the night before. Over their morning whisky, they were reminded by Papá not to forget to come to 719 Broadway that evening.

And, as Mamá served their bread and coffee, their eggs and ham, it was further emphasized that supper would be at the usual six o'clock, sharp.

The last skillet was barely dried when the movers arrived in the kitchen. And, once she was convinced that they were indeed responsible fellows, Mamá, accompanied by Antonia and Paca, Marty and Luis, walked up Broadway to Hotel Español.

Mamá barely had time to explore her new domain and check the supplies that Papá had already stocked, when the movers arrived; deposited the pots and pans, skillets, bowls, casseroles, plates, glasses, and cutlery; then were immediately gone for another load.

All day Hotel Español filled with the personal possessions of La Vaporina, including five seaman's trunks awaiting their owners' return.

And, late that afternoon, when the heavy fog tumbled over the western hills to remind one that summer was almost over, the boarders came home. There was Papá, setting up glasses behind his fine new bar. And there was Mamá, giving the final seasoning to the big pot of soup, the kettle of oxtails, and the pans of roasting chickens.

The boarders explored the new dining room, the new kitchen, and their own new rooms above. They crowded around the bar. And as the regular diners began to assemble—and new ones, too—glass after glass was raised; *botas* were passed from hand to hand.

"*Osagarria!*"—"Good life!" And Papá, hurrying from kitchen to dining room to bar, surveying his family and his friends, knew that this was, truly, the good life.

❋ ❋

Then. It was all so fast it was as though it had been overnight—the good life came to an end.

True, there had been talk of influenza—even of an epidemic. There had been stories in the newspapers and pictures of people with gauze bandages over their noses and mouths. Mamá, who could read only a little English, studied the pictures. She had a strange sense of foreboding and made little gauze masks for Marty and Luis.

Days passed. Perhaps the epidemic had decided not to come to Hotel Español? Then, one morning, a boarder failed to come down to breakfast. Papá hurried upstairs and when he came back his face was very serious. It was late afternoon before the doctor could come and, in the meantime, two more boarders had come home from work and fallen into their beds.

One after another, the boarders came down with the flu. The epidemic had indeed hit Hotel Español with full force.

There was some talk of sending the men to the hospital, but Mamá frowned at this. "No, no. The hospitals are too crowded. There will be no one to look after them. So they must stay here and I will take care of them."

So Mamá, with Antonia's help, added nursing to her regular routine. She measured medicine and saw to it that every drop was swallowed. She plumped pillows and sponged feverish faces. She served endless bowls of hot broth, spooning it into the mouths of her patients who were too weak to feed themselves. She spent untold hours at bedsides, talking life back into the men who were dying.

In all, she had fourteen patients.

And, when it was all over, she had lost only one. "You did much better than I," said the doctor, and he shook her hand, wondering at the strength and faith of this little woman.

So, a month later—with the flu epidemic certainly a thing of the past—there was no undue concern when four-year-old Luis woke from his nap hot and whimpering. But during the evening his temperature continued to rise, and Papá called the doctor.

No—no. It was not the flu. This the doctor knew. But just what it was—pneumonia? No. A touch of colic, perhaps.

Mamá sat by Luis's bed all night. And all the next day. The doctor came and went. Papá turned the bar over to Santiago and the kitchen to Paca and Antonia. Then he, too, went to sit by Luis.

Did the hours drag on—or did they happen all at once? Was the bar crowded—or was it empty? Was breakfast served? Dinner? Yes? No? Who could tell?

At four o'clock—or was it five? or six? or even that day?—there were two short muffled sobs, sounding as one, from Luis's room.

Baby Luis was dead.

CHAPTER 7

Papá Buys Sheep

Basoa ta ibaia auzo; au ezduen etxea gaizto.
El bosque y el rio, vecinos; casa sin ellos esta mal.
The forest and river, neighbors; a house without them is in trouble.

The move to Hotel Español five years ago had meant not only a new location, but a new guest list. At La Vaporina, most of the boarders and casual diners had been Galacian sailors, with—occasionally— Basque lumbermen or miners. Now, more and more of the guests were Basque sheepherders. And now there were women, too.

95

For San Francisco had not come by its title, The City, by accident. Indeed, it had always been—and still was—the hub of California-Nevada activity. And, like San Francisco, Hotel Español was the hub of Basque sheepherder activity.

Sheep had moved into California along with the missions, the original flock settling in San Diego in 1769. One hundred years later the first Basque sheepherders had begun to arrive, and they continued to come to California in ever-increasing numbers.

Masters of solitude, they would spend years alone on the vast ranges and foothills of California and Nevada. But, eventually, they would come to San Francisco. And it was inevitable that most of them would gravitate to Hotel Español.

"*Hola,* Papá. I have now, since spring, these papers from the Spanish consul. What should I do? What do you advise?"

"Papá, I bring to you and Mamá my wife. She is now with child and cannot stay alone on the ranch. When the baby comes you will take my wife to the hospital, no? Here is money. You will take good care of her, so I leave her with you. No, no, I cannot stay longer."

Papá understood. For how many years had he taken women heavy with child to the hospital? For how many years had he sat, clasping the work-worn hands of men recovering from surgery? For how many years had Mamá carried pots of hot broth to these hospitalized friends?

"Papá, I have been in the Sierra eight years now. A big herd—some money saved, too. It is time, do you think, to send for my sweetheart? A man gets no younger, Papá . . . a woman neither. It is a long time. But, perhaps, I should not send for her yet. Perhaps in another year—or two—after I build a larger flock—"

Papá's eyes twinkled. "Let a Basque get one ram and ten ewes and ten years later he'll wind up with a herd of 20,000." Then his voice became serious as he began to weigh the young man's questions and consider the best decision.

96

So, there was always talk of sheep. One day Chet Wing, secretary of the California Wool Growers Association, dropped by for lunch. The next day he brought his family to dinner, and from then on Hotel Español became his second home. He brought sheepmen from Australia and New Zealand, professors of animal husbandry from the universities, and the Secretary of Agriculture from Washington.

Mr. Wing always ordered lamb and managed to inveigle Mamá into serving more lamb courses than were generally on the menu. He and Papá became good friends—and they always talked sheep.

Papá joined the Wool Growers Association, and the more he read and the more he talked the more interested he became in owning sheep of his own.

It was not that the thought of quitting the hotel ever entered Papá's head. For, to him, his place was behind the bar—greeting his friends; welcoming strangers so that they would immediately feel at home; helping the herders, many of whom spoke no English and were bewildered by business technicalities and medical details.

Papá's life was the good life. Yet—listening to the talk of sheep. . . . Sometimes his thoughts wandered back to Navarre—to the rolling grazing lands of the Pyrenees foothills, the sheep-bells' clear tinkling, the dogs' short disciplined barks, the sweet smell of newborn lambs. Nostalgia? A small empty place that needed filling?

One day, as the sun was just rising over the Coast Range, Papá took the ferry to Oakland and boarded the little train with worn red plush seats—the little train that clattered along through vast fields of poppy and lupine until it reached Sacramento.

Papá returned to the hotel that evening. His face was flushed, and his eyes were excited. He had a little bouquet of wild flowers for Mamá. Also, he had news.

Over a late supper in the kitchen he told Mamá of his day. Of the little towns in the Sacramento Valley. Of the rich grasslands and clear streams. Of the ranch of Santiago Marco. Of the bands of fat sheep. And—of his plans to go into partnership with Mr. Marco.

It was an ideal arrangement, Papá said. Most of the sheep were in Yolo County west of Sacramento. And there were over a thousand head in the Livermore Valley southeast of Oakland. Neither location was far from San Francisco. Papá and his nephew, Pedro, together would buy a half interest. Mr. Marco would run the sheep business. Pedro would be a sheepherder. And Papá would remain at Hotel Español, but—in addition—would have a real part in California's sheep industry.

It was decided, and so it was done. And, until he sold out his share of the partnership in 1940, Papá took an active role in this industry.

He loved the trips to the country. He walked through the deep grass. He heard the crunch of dried live-oak leaves under his boots. He stood in the corrals at shearing time, wondering at the dexterity necessary to so neatly cut away the thick wool. He gave a hand during lambing, when the weather invariably turned cold and wet. He carried orphaned lambs inside his jacket. He learned to slip the skin from a still-born lamb over an orphan's head and gently persuade a bleating ewe that this baby was her own offspring.

In the evenings Papá walked into the sheepherder camps, each so neat one would think the men were about to stand military inspection. Around the camp fire, the herders would share their *botas* of wine and their food with Papá.

There were always stories. Of the old Castilian custom of *transhumante* flocks. In California, until the advent of the Forest Reserve in the late 1800's—after lambing, shearing, and dipping were completed and the grass in the lower altitudes had dried—hundreds of bands of sheep would be driven to the Sierra to graze for four to six weeks. The belief was that mountain grazing increased the wool clip one-and-a-half pounds per head, and the men could argue this point for hours.

Some of the older sheepherders remembered the *transhumante* flocks well and delighted in telling the young boys tales of fierce grizzly bears and of sleeping at corral entrances on *tapestras* (high platforms) that the bears could not climb.

But the favorite stories of the old days usually had to do with the five-cents-per-head tax that counties would levy on the bands being driven to and from the Sierra. And how the Basques would drive half their sheep through during the daylight, dutifully paying the tax, and then return after nightfall to smuggle through the rest.

Warmed by the food, the wine, and the stories, Papá would roll up in his canvas and sleep under the stars.

But, after a few days, his thoughts would be on Hotel Español. Was Santiago taking care of the bar? Was a friend waiting to discuss some important personal matter? Was Marty being a good boy at school— was he helping Mamá in the kitchen every afternoon? And Louise, the baby—was she growing so fast he would not recognize her? And Mamá. Ah, Angelita. Suddenly he missed her fearfully.

It was time to go home.

Carne (Meat)

For centuries sheep raising has been the primary industry in the Basque country. This accounts for the fact that, among Basques, lamb is a universal favorite. In the high pastures of the Pyrenees the sheep-herders often roast lamb over an open fire of aromatic wood—rosemary or bay. In the kitchens of the villages and cities the women prepare lamb several times a week, using less rustic—though equally delicious —recipes.

Veal and pork run close seconds to lamb in popularity. But both are often expensive, so the Basque housewife has developed a number of ways to prepare nutritious and economical variety meats.

Whatever the choice, the cooking is always done so that the true flavor of the meat dominates the dish. And, if a second meat (such as *chorizo* [pages 126–128] or ham) is used, it is added as a subtle complement.

Good beef is almost unheard of in the Basque provinces. And Mamá, though she learned to like beef, seldom served it at Hotel Español. "It is not Basque," she would say.

CORDERO (*Lamb*)

Chuletas de Cordero (*Lamb Chops*)

      12 lamb chops
       1 tablespoon olive oil
       1 medium onion
       1 bell pepper
       2 cloves garlic
       2 large tomatoes or 1½ cups
          solid pack tomatoes
      salt and pepper

Sprinkle the lamb chops with salt and pepper and brown well in hot oil. Place the chops in an ovenproof pan and keep them warm. Chop the onion, pepper, and garlic fine and fry them golden in the pan the chops were browned in. Peel and quarter the tomatoes and stir them into the other vegetables. Season with additional salt and pepper; simmer and stir the sauce for 5 minutes or so. Pour the sauce over the chops and cover the baking dish. Bake for 20 minutes in a 350° oven. Serves 6.

Chuletas de Cordero con Ajo (Lamb Chops with Garlic)

This delicious and simple recipe merely calls for making a little slit in each lamb chop and inserting a sliver of peeled garlic. The chops are then sprinkled with salt and pepper and fried in oil. The traditional accompaniment is *Pimientos Rojos* (page 186).

Chuletas de Cordero Asado (Lamb Chops, Roasted)

  12 lamb chops
   1 medium onion
   2 cloves garlic
  ¼ cup dry white wine*
  salt and pepper

Put the tiniest amount of water (¼ inch is sufficient) in the bottom of a shallow, ovenproof pan. Arrange the chops in the pan and sprinkle with salt and pepper. Peel and thinly slice the onion and garlic, and place the slices over the chops. Roast the chops in a 325° oven for 30 minutes. Now pour the wine over the chops and turn each one. Continue roasting for an additional 30 minutes, or until the chops are tender.

   *Dry red wine may be used instead, though the white is preferable.

   Sometimes Mamá cooked other vegetables, such as carrots or celery along with the meat—a highly recommended one-dish dinner. Serves 6.

Chilindron (*Lamb Stew*)

The addition of diced ham makes this dish particularly interesting. Be sure to serve mashed potatoes—the sauce is delicious and not one bit should be wasted.

3 pounds lamb stew meat	½ pound boiled ham
2 tablespoons olive oil	2 cups boiling stock or water
½ medium onion	1 cup dry red or white wine
2 cloves garlic	1 tablespoon tomato sauce
1 teaspoon salt	1 tablespoon minced parsley
¼ teaspoon pepper	

Lightly dust the lamb with flour and brown it well in hot oil. Mince the onion and garlic, and stir them into the meat with the salt and pepper. When the vegetables are barely tender, add the ham, cut in small pieces, and stir and fry until the ham begins to brown. Now pour in the stock or water, wine, and tomato sauce. Stir well and sprinkle with parsley. Cover and simmer for approximately one hour. Serves 6.

Guisado de Borreguito (*Lamb Stew*)

3 pounds lamb stew meat	1 teaspoon salt
flour	¼ teaspoon pepper
2 tablespoons olive oil	1 tablespoon tomato sauce
1 medium onion	½ cup dry red or white wine
2 cloves garlic	2 cups boiling water

Lightly flour the lamb, then brown it in oil. Chop the onion and garlic and stir into the meat, along with the salt and pepper. Cover the pot and allow the vegetables to brown for 3 or 4 minutes. Now stir in the tomato sauce, wine, and water. Allow the *Guisado* to come to a boil, cover, and reduce the heat. Simmer gently for a half-hour, or until the meat is tender. Serves 6.

That is the basic *Guisado de Borrequito*. But it can be varied in a number of ways. One or more vegetables—such as potatoes, carrots, peas, or string beans—can be simmered with the meat. A half cup of rice or paste (Mamá found rice especially to her liking) can be included instead of the vegetables. If either rice or paste is added, check the pot several times and add more hot water if necessary.

Cordero Cochifrito (Sautéed Lamb)

3 pounds lamb stew meat	¼ teaspoon pepper
2 tablespoons olive oil	1 tablespoon minced parsley
1 medium onion	juice of one-half lemon or
2 cloves garlic	1 tablespoon vinegar
1 teaspoon salt	

Dry the meat in paper towels and brown it in oil. Chop the onion and garlic well and add them to the meat. Alternately cover and uncover-and-stir the mixture until the vegetables are golden. Sprinkle in the remaining ingredients, cover, and simmer very slowly for about 30 minutes, or until the meat is tender. Serves 6.

Cochifrito is not a stew in the true sense of the word, for there is little liquid remaining when the meat is done.

Cordero Rehogado (Braised Leg of Lamb)

1 four- or five-pound leg of lamb	1 cup dry red or white wine
2 cloves garlic	1 onion
2 whole cloves (optional)	1 tomato
2 teaspoons salt	2 carrots
1 teaspoon pepper	6 medium potatoes

Peel the garlic and stick little slivers of it into the lamb. If the cloves are used, stick one in at each end of the roast, near the bone. (The cloves add a subtle flavor, and should not be passed over lightly.) Sprinkle the roast with salt and pepper and place it in a roasting pan to which a small amount of water (about one-quarter inch) has been added. Place the pan in a 325° oven. After about one hour, pour the wine over the meat and, from then until the roast is done, baste often. Add the vegetables about one hour before the roast is done. Cooking time for *Cordero Rehogado* is approximately 30 minutes to the pound, or a meat thermometer reading of 180°. Serves 6.

Cordero Asado—Hotel Español
(*Roast Leg of Lamb—Hotel Español Style*)

1 four- or five-pound leg of
  lamb
2 cloves garlic
2 teaspoons salt
½ teaspoon pepper

BASTING SAUCE
1 clove garlic
2 tablespoons vinegar
2 tablespoons vegetable oil

Peel the garlic and stick slivers of it into the lamb. Sprinkle the meat with salt and pepper and place it in a roasting pan in a 325° oven. Baste occasionally with a brush dipped into the garlic that has been mashed with the vinegar and oil. Cooking time is approximately 30 minutes to the pound, or 180° on a meat thermometer. When the roast is done, place it on a serving platter, and make gravy from the pan drippings. Serves 6.

Mamá usually served this *Cordero Asado* with a side dish of *Pimientos y Setas con Perejil* (page 186).

Cordero Asado de Maria Paz
(*Maria Paz' Roast Leg of Lamb*)

Papá's niece, Maria Paz, came to California from the little village of Oroz-Betelu high in the Pyrenees. She introduced Mamá to this method of roasting lamb, and it became a favorite at Hotel Español.

1 four- or five-pound leg of lamb	4 or 5 slices bacon
2 cloves garlic	1 teaspoon salt
	½ teaspoon pepper

Peel the garlic and cut it into thin slivers. Stick these into the roast. Dust lamb with salt and pepper. Fasten the bacon over the meat with toothpicks. Roast the lamb in a 325° oven for approximately 30 minutes to the pound, or until a meat thermometer reading of 180°. Serves 6.

Cordero Asado con Oregano
(*Roast Leg of Lamb with Oregano*)

1 four- or five-pound leg of lamb	2 cloves garlic
2 teaspoons salt	1 tablespoon olive oil
2 teaspoons crushed oregano leaves	

Mash one of the garlic cloves with the salt, oregano, and oil. Rub the outside of the roast with this mixture. Insert the other garlic clove near the bone. Roast in a 350° oven for 1½ hours. The outside should be crackling brown; the inside pink and tender. Serves 6.

Fritada de Borreguito (*Lamb Shoulder*)

4 pounds lamb shoulder stew
  meat
1 small onion
2 cloves garlic
1 bell pepper

2 whole cloves
1 #303 can solid pack
  tomatoes
½ can tomato sauce
salt and pepper

Mince the onion and garlic. Coarsely chop the pepper. Mash the tomatoes. Put all the ingredients in a large pot over medium-high heat. Stir and mix until the lamb begins to brown. Now, with the heat turned to medium, allow the *fritada* to cook—uncovered, and with a good stir now and then—for about 30 minutes. Cover and simmer gently for an additional hour, with an occasional stir. Serves 4–6.

    Fritada de Borreguito is excellent served with rice.

CARNE DE VACA (*Beef*)

Carne Mechada (*Pot Roast*)

3 pounds beef pot roast
1 clove garlic
¼ cup olive oil
1 onion
2 carrots
¼ small can tomato sauce

3 cups stock or water
1 cup dry white wine
small bunch parsley
1 bay leaf
salt, pepper, and flour

Tie the pot roast so that it will retain its shape and rub it with salt, pepper, and flour. Heat the oil in a Dutch oven or heavy casserole and brown the meat well on all sides. Now add the onion, chopped, and the carrots, cut in chunks, along with all the other ingredients. Cover the

106

pot, reduce the heat, and simmer slowly for about 2½ hours. Serve with boiled potatoes or noodles. Serves 4–6.

Guisado de Carne (*Beef Stew*)

3 pounds beef stew meat	1 whole clove
¼ cup olive oil	1 tablespoon minced parsley
1 medium onion	potatoes, carrots, peas, small
1 clove garlic	artichokes, mushrooms, or
3 cups stock or water	string beans
½ cup red wine	salt, pepper, and flour

Dust the meat with salt, pepper, and flour. Brown in hot olive oil in a heavy casserole. Stir in the onion and garlic—both minced—and cook until the vegetables are golden. Now add the stock, wine, whole clove, and parsley. Cover and simmer slowly for about 2½ hours. Add your own choice of the suggested vegetables during the last half-hour. If potatoes are omitted, serve the *Guisado* with rice. Serves 6.

CARNE DE CERDO (*Pork*)

Chuletas de Cerdo con Espinacas (*Pork Chops with Spinach*)

4 large pork chops	1 tablespoon chopped onion
flour	¼ cup white wine
½ teaspoon salt	½ teaspoon prepared mustard
2 tablespoons oil	1 pound fresh spinach or
1 clove garlic	1 package frozen chopped
2 tablespoons minced parsley	spinach

107

Trim excess fat from the pork chops and dust them with flour and salt. Brown them well in hot oil, then cover and cook 10 minutes over low heat. Transfer the chops to a shallow casserole. Mince the garlic and add it, along with the parsley and onion, to the fat in which the chops were cooked. Stir and cook these vegetables until they are soft, then add the wine, mustard, and well-washed chopped spinach. Simmer for 5 minutes. Drain excess liquid and place the vegetables over the chops. Cover and bake 20 to 25 minutes at 375°. Serves 4.

Cerdo Asado (*Roast Loin of Pork*)

4 pounds loin of pork	1 carrot
2 cloves garlic	1 cup boiling water
3 whole cloves	½ cup dry red or white wine
3 tomatoes	salt and pepper
½ onion	

Peel the garlic, cut it in slivers, and stick it into the pork. Then rub the meat all over with salt and pepper, and stick one whole clove at each end and one in the top center. Place the meat in a roasting pan, arranging the cut-up vegetables around it. Put the pan in a 350° oven. When the meat begins to brown, add the boiling water and wine to the pan. Bake, uncovered, 30 to 35 minutes to the pound (185° on a meat thermometer), basting the roast occasionally. Serves 6–8.

Costillas de Cerdo (*Spareribs with Vegetables*)

Because the spareribs are nearly done before they are combined with the vegetables they will retain their delightful crispness.

4 pounds pork spareribs	4 medium potatoes
1 tablespoon olive oil	¼ cup tomato sauce
2 medium onions	1 cup boiling water
2 cloves garlic	salt and pepper
3 bell peppers	

Cut the spareribs in serving-size pieces and brown in hot oil. Reduce the heat and continue cooking and turning the ribs until they are crisp and nearly done (approximately 45 minutes). Remove the ribs and drain all but one teaspoon of the fat. Add the vegetables that have been cut in thick slices, and stir them until they are golden. Return the spareribs to the pan and pour the tomato sauce and boiling water over them. Season with salt and pepper. Cover the pan and simmer gently for 15 minutes, or until the vegetables are tender. Serves 4–6.

Jamón Frito con Tomates (Fried Ham with Tomatoes)

2 pounds sliced ham
1 tablespoon olive oil
1 #303 can solid pack tomatoes
1 clove garlic

Fry the ham in hot olive oil and, when it has browned nicely on both sides, remove it to a warm plate. Pour any excess fat from the pan, then add the tomatoes that have been pressed through a sieve, and the clove of garlic, well-mashed. Stir the sauce over low heat for 10 minutes. Return the ham to the sauce, cover, and cook slowly for an additional 10 minutes. Serves 4–5.

Chorizo con Patatas (Chorizo with Potatoes)

1 pound *chorizo* (pages 126–128)
4 medium-size potatoes
salt

Simmer the *chorizo* for 15 minutes to remove excess fat. While the *chorizo* are simmering, peel and quarter the potatoes. Drain the *chorizo* and cut them up or leave them whole. Place the meat and potatoes in a pan, add water just to cover, and boil until the potatoes are tender. Drain well, and season with a little salt. Serves 2–4.

CARNE DE TERNERA *(Veal)*

Chuletas de Ternera y Cerdo *(Veal and Pork Chops)*

Allow one veal chop and one pork chop for each person. Sauté the chops in olive oil with one whole clove garlic and a little salt and pepper. Remove the garlic before serving.

Simple? But each meat adds a bit of its own flavor to the other, and the final result is excellent.

Ternera con Jamón *(Veal with Ham)*

    3 pounds veal shoulder cut
      for stew
    3 slices boiled ham or
      prosciutto
    ¼ cup olive oil
    1 medium onion
    1 clove garlic
    ½ cup pitted ripe olives
    2 cups stock or water
    ½ cup dry white wine
    salt and pepper

Brown the veal in hot oil. Cut the ham in small pieces, and mince the onion and garlic. Add these, along with the other ingredients, to the veal. Season to taste with salt and pepper. Cover and simmer gently for one half-hour, or until the veal is tender. Serves 6.

Barquillos Rellenos (*Stuffed Veal Boats*)

16 slices veal for scallopini
5 slices boiled ham
4 hardboiled eggs
flour
¼ cup olive oil
1 medium onion
2 cloves garlic
1 cup water or stock
½ cup dry white wine
1 tablespoon tomato sauce
1 tablespoon minced parsley
1 4-ounce can mushrooms
salt and pepper

Slice the ham into strips and cut the eggs in quarters lengthwise. Roll 2 ham strips and 1 egg quarter in each slice of veal. Tie securely with string. Dust each veal roll with flour. Brown quickly in oil, turning so all sides are evenly browned. Place in a casserole.

In the same oil in which the veal was browned, sauté the garlic and onion—both minced. Add this to the veal rolls. Remove excess oil from the skillet. Then put the water or stock in the skillet and let it come to a boil, deglazing the pan. Add this liquid to the veal with the wine, tomato sauce, minced parsley, mushrooms with their juice, and salt and pepper to taste.

Let all ingredients come to a boil, then cover the casserole and simmer gently for about 30 to 40 minutes. Check occasionally to make sure the liquid has not evaporated. Add a little more water or stock if needed, but do not let the sauce become soupy. Remove strings from the veal rolls. Pour the sauce over them and serve. Serves 4.

Escalopes de Ternera (*Veal Scallops*)

This is a "Sunday Special" sort of dish!

12 slices veal for scallopini
12 slices boiled ham or
  prosciutto
¼ cup olive oil
1 medium onion

½ cup sherry
1 cup orange juice
1 teaspoon flour
salt and pepper

Place a slice of ham over each slice of veal. Pound together with a mallet or the edge of a plate. Roll up each ham-veal slice and fasten with toothpicks. Brown quickly in oil. Add the onion that has been finely chopped, the wine, and orange juice. Cover the pan and cook over low heat for about 25 minutes. Remove the meat to a hot platter. Thicken the remaining liquid with flour and season with salt and pepper. Pour the sauce over the veal and serve. Serves 6. (At Hotel Español, *Escalopes de Ternera* were usually served with buttered noodles.)

MENESTRA (*Basque Stew*)

Menestra is a marvelous Basque stew of various meats garnished with vegetables and hardboiled eggs. It is ideal for a large crowd.

Menestra

2 pounds veal stew meat
1 pound pork
1 frying chicken
¼ pound boiled ham
2 tablespoons olive oil
1 medium onion
1 clove garlic

1 2-pound can solid pack
  tomatoes
1 teaspoon minced parsley
12 cooked asparagus tips or
  artichoke hearts
6 hardboiled eggs
salt and pepper

Cut the pork and chicken in serving-size pieces and brown them, along with the veal, in oil. Mince the onion and garlic, add them to the meat, and cook until the vegetables are tender. Mash the tomatoes and stir them into the meat. Dice the ham and add it, along with the parsley, salt, and pepper. Add boiling water to cover the meat about a third of the way. Cover the pot and simmer the *Menestra* gently for an hour to 1½ hours. Check several times to be sure the liquid has not evaporated, but—at the same time—keep in mind that the final dish must not be soupy. Serves 12.

Serve the *Menestra* in a deep platter. Garnish it with hot asparagus tips or artichoke hearts and with halved hardboiled eggs.

CARNE MOLIDA (*Ground Meats*)

Pan de Carne (*Meatloaf*)

1½ pounds ground beef or
    equal parts beef, veal,
    and pork
½ medium onion
1 clove garlic
2 tablespoons minced
    parsley

½ cup breadcrumbs
1 egg
¼ cup milk
1 teaspoon salt
½ teaspoon pepper

Mince the onion and garlic. Mix all the ingredients thoroughly and pack gently into a loaf pan. Bake for one hour at 325°. At Hotel Español, *Pan de Carne* was usually served hot, with gravy made from the pan drippings. Sometimes, though, it was served cold, sliced very thin and garnished with sliced hardboiled eggs, pimientos, and parsley. Serves 4–6.

Pimientos Rellenos (*Stuffed Peppers*)

12 small bell peppers or
    canned pimientos
1½ pounds ground beef or
    equal parts of beef, veal,
    and pork
1 tablespoon olive oil
1 medium onion

2 cloves garlic
1 tablespoon minced parsley
1 cup soft breadcrumbs or
    cooked rice
1 teaspoon salt
½ teaspoon pepper

If fresh bell peppers are used, remove their stems and seeds and simmer in slightly salted water until they are just tender. If canned pimientos are used, simply dry them before stuffing.

To make the stuffing, brown the meat in oil, along with the onion and garlic, both minced. Cool slightly, add the other ingredients and mix well. Fill the peppers and place them in a roasting pan. Pour the sauce* over them and bake in a 350° oven until the tops are brown (about 30 minutes).

*Salsa (*Sauce*)

1 small onion
1 clove garlic
1 tablespoon minced parsley
1 cup stock or water
½ cup dry red wine
1 small can tomato sauce

Mince the onion and garlic and brown them in the skillet in which the meat mixture was prepared. Stir in the other ingredients and simmer for 10 to 15 minutes, or until the sauce is thickened. Mamá always liked a smooth sauce, so before pouring it over the peppers she would pass it through a sieve. This extra step is optional. Serves 6.

Albóndigas de Norine (Norine's Meatballs)

Use the same recipe as for appetizer *Albóndigas* (page 39), but make larger balls—about the size of ping-pong balls. Or, use this excellent recipe:

1 pound lean veal	½ teaspoon pepper
1 pound lean pork	1 tablespoon sugar
1 large onion	2 eggs
1 tablespoon chopped parsley	flour
½ loaf stale French bread	equal parts of oil and bacon
1 heaping teaspoon salt	fat or oil and butter

Have the butcher grind the veal and pork together. Put the meat in a large bowl. Peel and parboil the onion, chop it well, and add it to the meat, along with the salt, pepper, sugar, and parsley. Mix well. Moisten the bread with water or equal parts of water and milk, then squeeze it until it is almost dry. Add the bread to the meat, mix well; add the eggs, and mix well once more.

Using a light hand, form the meat mixture into small balls. (There will be approximately 30.) Roll them in flour, and fry in oil and bacon fat or oil and butter. When the meat balls are browned, place them in a casserole and cover with the following sauce:

Salsa (Sauce)

1 tablespoon olive oil	2 whole cloves
1 small onion	1 dried chili and a sprig
1 large clove garlic	each of parsley, celery,
1 heaping tablespoon flour	thyme, and a bay leaf
2 cups stock or 2 bouillon	½ teaspoon paprika
cubes dissolved in 2 cups	salt and pepper
of hot water	1 can sliced mushrooms
¼ can tomato sauce	

115

Chop the onion and fry it gently in oil. When the onion is half done add the chopped garlic and continue cooking until the vegetables are tender. Stir in the flour and, when it begins to bubble, add the hot stock and the other ingredients. Pour the sauce over the meatballs, cover the casserole and simmer, either on top of the stove or in a 350° oven, from 1½ to 2 hours. Check the casserole once or twice and add a little water if the sauce has evaporated too much. Add the mushrooms a half-hour before serving. Serves 6.

Albóndigas con Chorizo (*Meatballs with Chorizo*)

1 pound lean ground beef	2 slices bread
¼ pound *chorizo* (pages 126–128)	4 tablespoons olive oil
	flour
¾ teaspoon salt	½ cup sherry or dry white
1 tablespoon minced parsley	wine
1 egg	1 cup stock or water

Chop the *chorizo* well or put it through a grinder. Combine it with the ground beef, salt, and parsley. Soak the bread in water and squeeze dry. Add it, along with the egg, to the meat mixture. Make small balls and dust each with flour. Brown in hot oil. Add the wine and one cup stock or water. Cover and simmer for 20 to 30 minutes. Serves 4.

Patatas Rellenas (*Stuffed Potatoes*)

This is a marvelous way to glorify leftover poultry, meat, or even fish or shellfish.

6 nicely shaped baking potatoes	3 or 4 cups chopped leftover meat

4 tablespoons minced onion	2 tablespoons butter or olive oil
2 tablespoons minced parsley	2 eggs
2 tablespoons chopped pimientos	salt and pepper
	1 bunch parsley

Cut one end from each of the potatoes and scoop out the inside, leaving a shell of no more than one-third inch. (Save the scooped-out part for soup.) Cut a thin slice from the other end so that the shell will stand up.

Mince the onion and simmer it in one tablespoon butter or oil until it is barely tender. Add the minced parsley and pimientos, along with the chopped meat. Stir and cook for 3 or 4 additional minutes. Season to taste. Stuff the potato shells with the onion-meat mixture, packing firmly.

Beat the eggs, with a little salt, until they are thick. Heat the remaining butter or oil in a skillet. Dip each potato, top-side down, into the beaten egg and then into the hot oil just long enough to seal the opening. Return the potato to the beaten egg, rolling it around to coat completely; then roll the potato quickly in the hot oil just long enough to set the egg. Stand the potatoes up in a deep baking dish or kettle. Pour the following sauce over them (the sauce should cover the potatoes three-fourths of the way), and bake, uncovered, for 30 to 40 minutes at 375°, or until the potatoes are tender. Garnish with parsley.

Salsa (Sauce)

1 medium onion	1 bay leaf
1 tablespoon olive oil	1 4-ounce can sliced mushrooms (optional)
2 tablespoons flour	
2 cups light stock	1 tablespoon sliced pimiento (optional)
½ cup dry white wine	
1 tablespoon minced parsley	salt and pepper

Chop the onion very fine and fry it in olive oil until it is just golden. Stir in the flour, and when it bubbles up, add the stock and wine. Cook the sauce for a minute or two, or until it begins to thicken. Season to taste. Strain the sauce over the potatoes and add the parsley, bay leaf, mushrooms, and pimiento. (The exact amount of sauce necessary will vary with the size of the baking dish. Add more broth or water if there is not enough sauce.) Serves 6.

SOBRAS (Variety Meats)

Colas de Vaca Guisado (Oxtails)

2 oxtails (3 to 4 pounds)	4 whole cloves
1 tablespoon olive oil	4 carrots
1 clove garlic	4 medium potatoes
1 tablespoon flour	8 whole pearl onions
3 cups water	1 bell pepper
¼ cup dry red wine	1 tablespoon chopped parsley
½ cup tomato sauce	salt to taste
6 peppercorns	

Disjoint the oxtails and brown in oil in a Dutch oven. Mince the garlic and add it with the flour. Cook and stir for a few minutes. Then add the water, wine, tomato sauce, peppercorns, and cloves. Cover and simmer for 2 to 3 hours, or until the meat is tender. Add more water if the liquid has reduced too much. Cut up the carrots, potatoes, and pepper and add them, along with the onions and parsley, 30 minutes before serving. Serves 4.

Lengua de Vaca Con Salsa
(*Beef Tongue with Sauce*)

1 fresh beef tongue (4 to 5 pounds)	1 bunch parsley
	1 whole tomato
2 cloves garlic	1 teaspoon salt
2 stalks celery	2 peppercorns

Cover the tongue with cold water and let it come to a rolling boil. Remove the tongue and discard the water and any foam. Replace the tongue in the kettle, cover with fresh cold water, and bring to a boil again. Skim off any scum that appears. Add the vegetables, salt, and peppercorns; cover the pot and simmer over medium heat for 3 hours or until the tongue is tender.

Remove the tongue, but be sure to reserve the broth. Place the tongue in the sink and run cold water over it while removing all traces of skin and roots. Set the tongue aside and make the following sauce:

Salsa (*Sauce*)

2 tablespoons oil	½ small can tomato sauce
1 medium onion	½ cup tongue broth
1 clove garlic	pinch of oregano (optional)
1 bell pepper	1 tablespoon minced parsley
1 stalk celery	salt and pepper
1 #303 can solid pack tomatoes	

Chop the onion, garlic, bell pepper, and celery and brown them gently in oil. Mash the tomatoes and stir them in, along with the other ingredients. Cover the pan and simmer the sauce for about 45 minutes. Slice the tongue and heat it in the sauce before serving. Serves 8–10.

Strain the broth left from cooking the tongue and use it as stock to cook rice or pasta or as an excellent soup stock.

Lenguas de Cordero Salteadas
(Sautéed Lambs' Tongues)

2 pounds fresh lamb tongues	2 eggs
1 thick slice lemon	flour
¼ onion	1 tablespoon olive oil
1 teaspoon salt	

Put the tongues, lemon, onion, and salt in a kettle and cover with cold water. Simmer for 2 to 2½ hours or until the tongues are tender. Rinse the tongues in cold water and skin them. Slice crosswise in quarter-inch pieces. Beat the eggs well with a pinch of salt. Dip the meat slices in flour and then in the beaten eggs. Fry quickly in hot olive oil, turning to brown both sides. Serves 4–6.

Almost invariably, Mamá served a bowl of hot *Salsa de Codorniz* (page 189) with *Lenguas de Cordero*. The tongues are excellent, too, served with lemon wedges.

Lenguas de Cordero Con Salsa
(Lamb Tongues with Sauce)

2 pounds fresh lamb tongues
1 thick slice lemon
½ onion
1 teaspoon salt

Simmer, rinse, skin, and slice the tongues as directed in the recipe for *Lenguas de Cordero* (above). Arrange the slices of meat on a platter and keep them warm in the oven while you make this sauce:

120

Salsa (Sauce)

½ onion	mashed solid pack tomatoes
1 clove garlic	2 tablespoons parsley
1 tablespoon olive oil	1 tablespoon flour
¼ cup tomato sauce or	salt and pepper

To make the sauce, mince the onion and garlic and fry them in olive oil until they are golden. Stir in the flour, and when it has bubbled up, add the tomato sauce and parsley. Season with a little salt and pepper. Simmer the sauce for 5 minutes and pour it over the sliced tongue. Serves 4–6.

Sometimes Mamá heated pitted black olives or tinned artichoke hearts in their own juices, drained them, and arranged them in the center of the tongue slices just before she added the sauce.

Riñones Salteados (Kidney Sauté)

4 baby beef kidneys	2 tablespoons chopped
1 tablespoon bacon fat	parsley
1 small onion	½ to ¾ cup dry red wine
1 clove garlic	½ to ¾ cup water
1 heaping tablespoon flour	paprika
2 whole cloves	salt and pepper
¼ teaspoon crushed thyme leaves	

Wipe the kidneys well, cut out the fibers, and remove all traces of fat. Cut the kidneys in small squares and pat dry with paper towels. Sauté the kidneys in bacon fat over a low fire and, if any juice accumulates, drain it. Chop the onion and garlic and add them to the meat. Stir and

121

fry until the vegetables are golden. Stir in the flour, and allow it to brown. Now add the cloves, thyme, parsley, and paprika. Season to taste with salt and pepper, and pour equal parts of wine and water to just cover the meat. Cover the pot and simmer slowly for 1 hour. Serves 4.

Hígado con Salsa de Vino (*Liver in Wine Sauce*)

1½ pounds calf's liver, sliced	1 clove garlic
2 tablespoons olive oil	½ cup dry red wine
2 medium onions	salt and pepper

Cut the liver slices in two-inch pieces. Peel and slice the onions and mince the garlic. Heat the olive oil in a skillet and sauté the liver and onions for 5 minutes, stirring constantly. Add the minced garlic, wine, salt, and pepper; cover and cook over very low heat for 15 minutes. Check once or twice to see that the dish has not become too dry. Remove the liver to a platter and pour the wine sauce over it. Serves 4–6.

Corazónes de Cordero con Calabaza (*Lamb Hearts with Zucchini*)

2 pounds lamb hearts*	1 teaspoon salt
1 tablespoon olive oil	¼ teaspoon pepper
1 medium onion	½ cup dry red wine
2 cloves garlic	2 pounds zucchini

Wash and dry the hearts and trim away excess fat and tough membranes. Cut the heart in small pieces and brown in hot oil. When the meat is well-browned on both sides add the onion and garlic, finely

122

chopped. Stir and cook until the vegetables are golden. Season with salt and pepper and pour in the wine. Cover the pan and simmer the meat for 15 to 20 minutes or until it is tender. If the mixture seems too dry, a little water may be added.

Serve the meat and its juices over zucchini that has been sliced lengthwise and cooked separately in boiling salted water. Mamá usually served mashed or French fried potatoes with *Corazón*. Serves 6–8.

* Either beef or veal heart is equally delicious. Lengthen the cooking time by a good 10 minutes.

Sesos (Brains)

Excellent for Sunday breakfast!

2 pounds lamb, calf, or beef brains	2 eggs
1 teaspoon salt	2 tablespoons butter and 2 tablespoons olive oil
flour	lemon wedges
1 tablespoon lemon juice	parsley

Soak the brains in cold water for at least 20 minutes. Clean them thoroughly and drop into boiling water to which the salt and lemon juice have been added. Lower the heat and simmer gently. (Fifteen minutes for lamb brains, 20 minutes for calf, and 30 minutes for beef.) Plunge the brains into cold water for 15 minutes.

Pat the brains dry on paper towels and cut into serving-size pieces. Dip in flour and then into the eggs that have been beaten with a pinch of salt. Fry in butter and oil quickly until golden on one side; turn and allow the other side to brown. Serve immediately with lemon wedges and parsley. Serves 4–6.

123

Mollejas de Ternera (Sweetbreads)

Mamá would precook sweetbreads the same way she precooked brains. Then, often, she cut the sweetbreads in small pieces and added them to beef stock with, perhaps, a bit of rice or vermicelli. Sometimes she mashed the sweetbreads and mixed them with ground beef for meat patties. But the way Papá liked sweetbreads best was when she sautéed them with an equal quantity of sliced mushrooms, and just a hint each of minced onion, garlic, and parsley.

Patas de Cerdo con Tripa (Pigs' Feet with Tripe)

An outstanding dish!

4 pigs' feet
1 pound honeycomb tripe
1 large onion
1 clove garlic
½ lemon
1 bay leaf
3 whole peppercorns
3 whole cloves
1 teaspoon salt

Have the butcher cut the pigs' feet in half, lengthwise. Cover them with cold water, season with the onion, garlic, lemon, bay leaf, cloves, peppercorns, and salt. Simmer for 4 hours, drain, and reserve. The stock may be strained and chilled for pigs'-foot jelly.

Prepare the tripe by washing it well in several changes of cold water, and slicing it into bite-size pieces. Cover the tripe with cold water, add ½ teaspoon salt, and simmer for 2 hours. Drain well.

124

Salsa (Sauce)

1 tablespoon olive oil
1 medium onion
1 clove garlic
1 bell pepper
2 whole cloves

1 small can tomato sauce
1 #303 can solid pack
  tomatoes
1 tablespoon parsley
salt and pepper

Begin to prepare the sauce a good hour before serving time. Dice the onion, garlic, and bell pepper and simmer them in olive oil until the vegetables are golden. Stir in the tomato sauce and the tomatoes that have been pressed through a sieve. Sprinkle in the parsley and cloves. Add the tripe, stir well, and place pigs feet on top. Cover and simmer gently for an hour. Remove the cloves before serving. (If they can be located!) Serves 8.

Patas de Cerdo con Tripa should always be accompanied by a bowl of garbanzos (page 162).

Patas de Cerdo Dulces (Glazed Pigs' Feet)

6 pigs' feet
1 cup flour, approximately
2 eggs

3 tablespoons olive oil
3 tablespoons sugar

Cook the pigs' feet as for Patas de Cerdo con Tripa (page 124). Reserve 2 cups broth. Cool the pigs' feet and remove the larger bones.

Have the flour ready, beat the eggs, and heat the olive oil in a skillet. Dip the pigs' feet in flour, then in the egg. Fry until browned on both sides. Place the pigs' feet in a baking pan, sprinkle them with sugar, and pour the sauce around them. Bake at 350° for 30 minutes, or until pigs' feet are nicely glazed. Baste two or three times. Serve Patas de Cerdo Dulces with mashed potatoes.

Salsa (Sauce)

1 tablespoon olive oil	2 cups broth
½ medium onion	1 tablespoon minced parsley
2 cloves garlic	salt and pepper
1 tablespoon flour	

To make the sauce, mince the onion and garlic and simmer them in olive oil until they are golden. Stir in the flour and allow it to brown. Add the broth, stirring rapidly so that the sauce does not lump. Sprinkle in the parsley and season with salt and pepper. Simmer *Salsa* for 5 minutes before adding it to the pigs' feet. Serves 6.

CHORIZO (Spanish Sausage)

Chorizo, pork sausage seasoned with garlic and Spanish paprika, plays an important part in Basque cooking.

The sausages are available in some markets, or you can make them yourself. When you do, you'll be involved in an age-old culinary art—sausages being one of the earliest forms of processed food.

Rita Rodriguez supervised our first *chorizo*-making session. Like Mamá and Papá, Rita came from Spain to San Francisco where she and her husband owned first a boarding house and later a restaurant. As a young girl in the Spanish province of Asturias, she had worked as assistant to a *chorizera,* a little woman who went from house to house, preparing and storing a variety of sausages and cured meats for each family. In San Francisco, Rita continued making her own sausages and curing her own meats. Why? "Because they are better."

Chorizo-making simply involves mixing ground pork with a hand-

ful of seasonings and pressing the meat mixture into casings. Rita
Rodriguez uses a sausage press, but a metal cooky press (3-cup capacity)
will do. However, with a cooky press, you will have to work with shorter
pieces of casing.

Casings are available from the butcher, although a few days notice
is often necessary. Get the medium (one-and-one-fourth-inch diameter)
size.

Chorizo

6 pounds lean pork shoulder	¾ teaspoon oregano
5 or 6 large garlic cloves	¾ teaspoon thyme
1 tablespoon salt	1½ teaspoons black pepper
½ teaspoon crushed chilis	¼ cup dry white wine
¼ cup Spanish paprika*	medium-size sausage casings
½ teaspoon saltpeter	and string

*Imported Spanish paprika is usually available in Spanish or
Mexican groceries or in specialty food shops. Several American spice
companies also process and package Spanish paprika. The latter
product, however, lacks the zip of the imported variety, so it will be
necessary to increase the amount used.

Have your butcher grind the meat, using a coarse blade. Peel and slice
the garlic. Place it in a mortar with the salt and pound to a fine paste.
(Or the garlic, salt, and wine can be whirled in an electric blender.)
Put the ground meat on a bread board and sprinkle the garlic paste,
along with all the other ingredients, over it. Mix and knead *well*—
15 minutes is not too long. Pack the meat mixture into a bowl; cover
with waxed paper, and refrigerate 24 to 48 hours.

Stuffing the sausage casings takes time, so plan ahead.

On the day you are going to press the *chorizo* into the casings,
knead the meat mixture well again. Then fry a sample and taste for

127

seasoning. Sometimes a bit more salt is needed—or paprika—for the flavor of Spanish paprika is what makes these sausages distinctive.

Before using the casings, soak them briefly in lukewarm water and cut into two-foot lengths. Fit one end of the casing over a water faucet and run lukewarm water through. Press out excess water. The casing is now ready to fill.

Slip one end of the casing over the nozzle of a sausage or cooky press, sliding all the casing over the nozzle until only an inch is left free beyond the tip. Press the *chorizo* mixture into the casing, holding one hand gently around the nozzle so that the sausage plumps up.

If a casing breaks (and they do), simply cut the casing with a scissors at the point of the break and set the filled section of casing aside. Then pull about an inch of casing beyond the tip of the nozzle and start the filling process again.

To separate the *chorizo* into links, tie each end of the filled casing with fine string; then tie the ends together so that you have a ring. Now tie the sausages into links of approximately 5 inches each, leaving them in a ring. Prick each link three or four times with a darning needle. Mend any small breaks in a casing with patches cut from leftover casing.

Hang the *chorizo* rings in a cool airy place to dry for seven to ten days. They may then be stored in the refrigerator for up to two weeks or in the freezer for six months. Or (and this is Rita Rodriguez' method) pack the *chorizo* in jars or crocks and cover *completely* with a good vegetable oil. They will keep for six months.

There is no substitute for *chorizo* in Basque cooking. If you use garlic sausages or smoky links you will have a good dish, but it will not be Basque. But, if *chorizos* are unavailable in your area and you don't want to make the sausages yourself, there is one alternative.

Prepare a small quantity of *chorizo* stuffing, wrap in waxed paper and refrigerate for 2 or 3 days; fry a sample and taste for seasoning— then either use the whole batch within the next day or two or make small patties, wrap, and freeze. Before using *chorizo* patties that have been refrigerated or frozen, fry them slowly to remove excess fat.

CHAPTER 8

Prohibition

Ardo gozoak lau begi ta onikes.
El vino tiene cuatro ojos y no pies.
Wine has four eyes and no feet.

North Beach, 1919. Russian Hill sheltered it on the west. To the north was Fisherman's Wharf and the crab fleet. The eastern limit was the decaying, but still notorious, Barbary Coast. And pressed against the southern perimeter was Chinatown. North Beach, a polyglot mingling of Italian, French, and Basque, was Papá's home.

Everyone along Broadway, and along Columbus, as well as along the little residential streets that branched off from these two main arteries, drank wine with his meals. And all the men had a glass of whisky before dinner—with the Basques drinking a whisky before breakfast, too.

There was no drunkenness; the alcohol was part of a good diet. It gave a sharper appetite and allowed for better digestion.

So, when Papá opened the newspaper one morning and read about the Volstead Act, it was with considerable concern that he realized the Eighteenth Amendment had teeth in it. Prohibition had really come!

Slowly he carried the paper into the bar-room where Santiago was already having his coffee and whisky. Together the men read about the new act and tried to decide what to do.

"It is the law. Right here it tells it very clearly." Papá sighed. "But the boarders—we have, after all, a contract with them: a room, three meals, two bottles of wine, and two glasses of whisky each day." He shook his head. "Can even the government of the great United States ask a Basque to break a contract?

"It is a law—but not a natural law—not a good law. And can a man respect a law unless it is good? No. And if a man respects such a law can he longer respect himself? And," his voice was rising, "if a man can not respect himself who, then, will respect *him*?"

Santiago nodded. The men finished their coffee and whisky in silence. Their minds were made up.

During that day and several to follow, Papá and Santiago talked with other hotel-keepers, other owners of taverns and restaurants in North Beach. Mamá was apprehensive, but Papá tried to calm her fears. "It is," he chuckled, "as if all of North Beach is thinking like a true Basque."

Where bottles of whisky and brandy had stood proudly on the back-bar shelves, bowls of oranges and lemons were now arranged.

130

Papá carefully packed away the *botas* and the whisky glasses and replaced them with bottles of fruit juice and water tumblers. Then, armed with a lemon squeezer and a bowl of sugar, he began to train himself in the art of making fruit punch. . . .

Now, when the boarders came down to breakfast, they no longer stopped at the bar, but went right into the dining room. There, at each place, were two cups, one of each pair already holding the morning whisky.

Dinner was more complicated. There had to be a third cup for wine. Mamá frowned about the whole thing. But all she said was that there would have to be either an additional dishwasher or additional cups.

When Papá and Santiago returned from the restaurant supply house on Mission Street, Papá's eyes were merrier than usual. "Listen, Mamá, to what we have heard. That more cups have been sold in a month than were sold during all of last year! Many restaurants must be opening, no? Your cooking will have some strong competition."

Mamá smiled at the joke, but it was not this imaginary competition that worried her.

Strangers began to come to Hotel Español. Were they good citizens who merely wanted one of Mamá's fine dinners? Were they rounders, out on the town in search of a new speakeasy? Were they Federal investigators—sniffing out any suggestion of alcohol?

Papá put a lock on the dining-room door.

It was Papá's job to weigh the integrity of each new guest. "I am not running a speakeasy," he told Mamá firmly. "I believe, as I always have, that 'Wine has four eyes and no feet.' But that has never been true in our house. We must take care of our regular guests, and it is my responsibility to see that they get only the best."

But Mamá continued to worry, and once she had a real scare.

At the bar Papá was concocting his fruit punches. In the dining

131

room the boarders and the regular dinner patrons were eating their appetizers and bread, and drinking their whisky or wine from the new china cups. Mamá looked through the kitchen door to gauge how soon to fill the soup tureens. She smiled at the familiar faces, the warm conversation, the snatches of laughter.

Then suddenly, starting with the diners nearest the bar, there was a tense silence. Strange voices from the bar. Men's voices. Hard, firm, unyielding. Papá's voice—calm, friendly, but equally unyielding.

Next to Mamá, Santiago appeared as from nowhere. The waitress began collecting cups; the dishwasher, Santiago, and Mamá hurried to help.

The diners, haltingly at first, resumed their conversation. Then, like actors, attacked their appetizers with apparent gusto.

Down the sink went the cups of wine and whisky. Down the sink went a full jug of wine, newly uncorked.

"Hurry. They have axes. Hurry, put the cups in the dishwater. Hurry. Serve the soup. Axes! Oh, poor Papá."

Mamá was busily dishing up platters of *garbanzos* when she heard the bolt turn on the dining-room door. The strange hard voices came nearer, and there were men—tall and strong and glowering—who really *did* carry axes. They rummaged through the pantry, the icebox, the cupboards, the shelves. They thumped down the basement stairs and moved the trunks and supplies that were stored there. They sifted through the garbage cans in the alley.

Then they were gone.

Mamá began heaping plates with chicken and platters with fish. Papá came in and put his arm around her shoulder. *"Más vale ser cabeza de ratón que cola de león."* ("Better to be the head of a mouse than the tail of a lion.") He repeated the old proverb lightly and with an edge of laughter.

But when Mamá pressed her cheek against his she saw that his forehead was beaded with perspiration.

132

Aves Caseras (Poultry)

There was one thing about American markets that Mamá was never able to understand. They always had plenty of chickens, ducks, and rabbits. And, in winter, there were geese and turkeys—the latter quite strange to her. But where were all the game birds: the partridges and quail, pigeons, pheasants, and doves? Papá went to great lengths to explain the laws that controlled the killing of game birds and prohibited their sale. But Mamá still felt it was a terrible shame that the eating of these birds was limited only to hunters and their close friends.

Autumn was the time when she could least tolerate this strange law. For in the Pyrenees in autumn doves migrate through the narrow passes and are snared in huge nets. Ah, how well she remembered the markets then, with tray after tray full of those delectable birds. Papá liked to tease her: "But now you have something new—turkey. See, it is a very American bird: so big. Why one turkey would make two dozen of the doves. What do you think of that?"

But Mamá was not so easily appeased. And, it was not until the introduction of Cornish game hens that she found any real consolation.

POLLO Y AVES SILVESTRES
(Chicken and Game Birds)

Pollo Frito (Fried Chicken)

This is a typically Basque method of cooking chicken. It is simple, and no other flavor is allowed to intrude. The chickens must be young

133

—only 1¼ to 1½ pounds each—and the clove of garlic must be small. Just enough to point up the flavor of the chicken.

Allow one-half chicken for each serving.

1 1¼–1½ pound split fryer
1 tablespoon olive oil
1 small clove garlic
salt and pepper

Dry the chicken well, sprinkle with salt and very little pepper. Place, skin side down, in hot fat and fry golden brown. Turn the halves, lower the heat, and drop the garlic clove into the pan. Cover and continue to cook until the chicken is tender (about 20 minutes). Remove the garlic before serving. Serves 2.

Pollo Frito con Patatas (*Fried Chicken and Potatoes*)

This is another beautifully simple chicken dish, one in which the potatoes fry right along with the chicken. Mamá preferred to rub the chicken with a thin coating of lard. Shortening can be substituted.

1 2-pound frying chicken
lard or shortening
4 medium potatoes
salt and pepper

Cut the chicken in serving-size pieces, drying each piece and rubbing all sides with a thin coating of lard or shortening. Brown the pieces slowly in a skillet over medium heat. When the chicken is nicely brown, add the potatoes, peeled and thinly sliced. Shake the pan to distribute the potatoes and season with salt and a little pepper. Cover the pan partially and continue cooking, over low heat, for 20 to 30 minutes, or until both the chicken and potatoes are tender. Shake the pan two or three times during the cooking, or carefully turn the chicken and potatoes with a fork. Serves 4.

Pollo Salteado (Chicken Sauté)

1 2-pound frying chicken	½ cup mushrooms
1 tablespoon olive oil	½ cup dry white wine
½ clove garlic	salt and pepper
1 teaspoon parsley	

Cut the chicken in serving-size pieces and brown lightly in oil. Mince the garlic and add it to the chicken. Drain any excess oil, add all the other ingredients, and season to taste. Cover the pan and cook the chicken slowly, 20 to 30 minutes, or until it is tender. Serves 4.

Pollo Guisado (Chicken Stew)

2 1½-pound fryers	1 can sliced pimientos
2 tablespoons olive oil	½ cup dry white wine
½ medium onion	pinch saffron
1 clove garlic	salt and pepper
1 tablespoon parsley	

Cut the fryers into serving-size pieces, and dry well. Heat the oil in a casserole or deep skillet, and brown the chicken on all sides. Peel and mince the onion and garlic and add them, along with the parsley, pimientos, saffron, salt and pepper. Pour in the wine, adding just enough boiling water to half-cover the chicken. Simmer, covered, 30 to 40 minutes, or until the chicken is tender. Serves 4–6.

Sometimes Mamá added potato balls, quartered potatoes, artichoke hearts, or mushrooms during the last 15 minutes of cooking.

135

Pollo Vascongado (Chicken Basque Style)

This is an outstanding dish, and diners at Hotel Español asked for it again and again. Mamá usually served it on Sundays.

1 2-pound frying chicken	1 cup dry white wine
1 tablespoon olive oil	½ pound large shelled shrimp
1 medium onion	¼ teaspoon paprika
½ cup diced boiled ham	1 tablespoon minced parsley
1 clove garlic	salt and pepper to taste

Cut the chicken in serving-size pieces, dry well, and dust lightly with flour. Heat the oil in a casserole or deep skillet and brown the chicken well on all sides. Remove the chicken and add the onion and garlic, minced, and the ham to the fat that remains in the pan. Stir the vegetables and ham so they will cook evenly; and, when they are tender, stir in the wine, shrimp, paprika, and parsley. Replace the chicken, sprinkle with a little salt and pepper, cover, and simmer 30 to 45 minutes, or until the chicken is tender. Serves 4.

Pollo con Jamón (Chicken with Ham)

1 2-pound frying chicken	¼ cup dry white wine
1 tablespoon olive oil	¼ pound boiled ham
½ small onion	salt and pepper
1 clove garlic	½ cup pitted olives (optional)
¼ bell pepper	
1 medium tomato or ½ cup solid pack tomatoes	

Cut the fryer in serving-size pieces and brown in hot oil. Chop the vegetables (except for the tomatoes) and add them to the chicken.

When the vegetables are tender stir in the tomatoes that have been mashed, the wine, and the cut-up ham. Season to taste, cover, and cook gently for about 45 minutes or until the chicken is tender. Serves 4.

Pollo con Garbanzos y Pimientos
(Chicken Roasted with Garbanzos and Peppers)

1 3-pound roasting hen	2 cups cooked *garbanzos* (page 162)*
1 tablespoon olive oil	4 bell peppers
2 cloves garlic	salt and pepper

Peel the garlic cloves and put them inside the chicken with a little salt and pepper. Skewer or tie the bird and rub all over with olive oil, salt, and pepper. Place the bird in a roasting pan. Roast for 2½ hours, or until the chicken is tender. An hour before the bird is done drain excess fat and arrange the *garbanzos,* along with a little of their cooking liquid, around the chicken. Seed and quarter the peppers and place them over the *garbanzos* 30 minutes before the chicken is done. Serves 4–6.

　* If canned *garbanzos* are used, simmer them for 15 minutes with 1 small clove of garlic, minced, 2 tablespoons minced onion, and 1 tablespoon tomato sauce.

Pollo Asado (Roast Chicken)

1 3-pound roasting hen	1 stalk celery
1 tablespoon olive oil	1 carrot
1 clove garlic	½ cup dry white wine
1 small onion	salt and pepper

Place the garlic, onion, celery, and carrot in the chicken and tie or skewer the wings and legs. Rub the oil on the chicken and dust with salt and pepper. Put the chicken in a roasting pan and pour a little

137

water around it. Roast in a 325° oven for 2½ hours, or until the chicken is tender. After the first half-hour pour the wine into the pan. Serves 4.

Sometimes Mamá would roast potatoes along with the chicken. And she usually served roast chicken with *Pimientos y Setas con Perejil* (page 186).

Hígados de Pollo (*Chicken Livers Sauté*)

1 pound chicken livers	1 teaspoon parsley
1 tablespoon olive oil	½ cup sliced mushrooms
1 clove garlic	(optional)
½ cup dry white wine	salt and pepper

Quickly brown the livers and the minced garlic in oil. Add the wine, parsley, and mushrooms. Season with salt and pepper. Cover the pan and simmer gently, shaking the skillet occasionally, for 3 minutes. Serve the chicken livers with rice. Serves 4.

When Cornish hens first came on the market in San Francisco, Papá quickly bought a case of them and hurried back to Hotel Español with his prize. Mamá was delighted, and in no time had remembered a handful of recipes for small game birds.

Gallinas de Cornvalles Asadas (*Roast Cornish Hens*)

4 Cornish hens or small chickens	¼ pound boiled ham
	2 cups dry white wine
1 tablespoon olive oil	1 cup water
1 medium onion	¼ cup white wine vinegar
4 cloves garlic	2 bay leaves
2 bell peppers	salt and pepper

Tie or skewer each hen so that the legs and wings will stay in place. Rub a little oil on each bird; place in a shallow roasting pan, and sprinkle with salt and pepper. Peel and cut up the onion and garlic and arrange them, along with the cut-up bell pepper and ham, around the hens. Pour in the wine, water, and vinegar; drop a bay leaf at each end of the pan, and roast in a preheated 375° oven for about 1 hour, basting often. Before serving, remove the bay leaves and untie the hen. Serves 4.

The juices and vegetables that remain in the pan can either be poured over the hens or used to make gravy for mashed potatoes or rice.

Gallinas de Cornvalles en Escabeche (*Marinated Cornish Hens*)

4 Cornish hens or small chickens	¼ teaspoon pepper
¼ cup lemon juice	½ teaspoon paprika
¼ cup olive oil	1 stalk celery
4 cloves garlic	1 carrot
1 teaspoon salt	½ cup dry white wine

Tie or skewer the hens so they will retain their shape. Mix together the lemon juice, oil, 2 cloves of the garlic (bruised), salt, pepper, and paprika. Marinate the hens for about an hour. Drain the hens and place them in a 400° oven. As soon as they begin to brown, remove any fat that has accumulated, and add the celery, carrot, and 2 cloves of garlic that have been chopped together. Pour the wine into the pan and continue cooking. The hens will be done in 45 minutes to an hour. Serves 4.

Sometimes, after the hens were marinated, Mamá would stuff them with *Relleno de Arroz Silvestre* (page 143).

Perdices en Salsa (Partridges in Gravy)

This is the traditional Basque way of preparing such game birds as partridges, quail, pigeons, doves, or pheasants. If no game is available, substitute Cornish hens. A rich gravy forms around the birds as they cook.

4 partridges	1 medium onion
¼ cup flour	3 cloves garlic
1 teaspoon salt	1 bunch parsley
⅛ teaspoon pepper	2 whole cloves
2 tablespoons olive oil	¼ cup vinegar

Wash the birds, dry them well, and tie or skewer so that the wings and legs will stay in place. Dust with flour, salt, and pepper. Heat the oil in a frying pan and brown the birds carefully along with the chopped onion and garlic. Place the birds and vegetables in a casserole, deglaze the pan with 2 cups boiling water, and add the liquid to the casserole. Add the remaining ingredients. Let the casserole come to a boil, lower heat, and simmer gently for 1 hour or until the birds are tender. Remove the parsley and cloves from the gravy before serving. Serves 4.
Perdices en Salsa is excellent with wild rice.

Perdices con Chocolate (Partridges with Chocolate)

Follow the recipe for *Perdices en Salsa*. When the birds are tender, remove them from the casserole and add 4 squares of unsweetened chocolate to the sauce in the pan. Stir over low heat until the chocolate has melted. Return the birds to the sauce and simmer gently for 5 minutes. Serves 4.

140

Perdices con Alcaparras (Partridges with Capers)

Like the preceding two recipes, this one can be used with any small game birds or Cornish game hens.

4 partridges
2 tablespoons olive oil
3 cloves garlic
1 bell pepper
1 medium onion
1 cup dry red or white wine

1 bay leaf
1 cup boiling water or broth
1 teaspoon vinegar
1 tablespoon capers
salt and pepper

Wash and dry the partridges, and either tie or skewer them. Heat the oil in a heavy pan and brown the birds lightly. Chop the garlic, bell pepper, and onion and add them, along with the other ingredients, to the pan. Salt and pepper to taste. Cover the pan and bake in a 350° oven for 1 hour or until the birds are tender. Serves 4.

CONEJO (Rabbit)

Conejo Frito (Fried Rabbit)

1 rabbit (1¼ to 1½ pounds)
2 tablespoons olive oil
¼ cup flour seasoned with
    salt and pepper
2 cloves garlic

Cut the rabbit in serving-size pieces, dust it with seasoned flour, and brown in hot oil. Peel the garlic cloves and toss them into the pan.

Cover, and cook slowly for 1 hour or until the rabbit is tender. Remove the garlic before serving. Serves 3–4.

Guisado de Conejo (*Stewed Rabbit*)

1 rabbit (1¼ to 1½ pounds)	2 whole cloves
¼ cup flour seasoned with	½ cup dry red or white wine
salt and pepper	½ can tomato sauce
2 tablespoons olive oil	½ cup mushrooms
1 medium onion	1 tablespoon parsley
2 cloves garlic	1 cup boiling water
1 bell pepper	

Cut the rabbit into serving-size pieces and dust with the seasoned flour. Brown the rabbit well in hot oil, and remove the pieces to a casserole. Chop the onion, garlic, and bell pepper; brown them lightly in the oil, and pour the vegetables over the rabbit, along with the other ingredients. Add boiling water just to cover the rabbit. Cover the casserole and simmer gently for about 1 hour, or until the rabbit is tender. Serves 3–4.

Potatoes or potatoes and peas can also be added to the stew for the last half-hour.

Conejo con Ternera (*Rabbit with Veal*)

1 rabbit (1¼ to 1½ pounds)	4 slices of veal scallops
flour	1 cup dry white wine
3 tablespoons olive oil	1 cup boiling water
3 cloves garlic	1 tablespoon parsley
½ medium onion	salt and pepper

Cut the rabbit in serving-size pieces, dust with flour, and brown in hot oil. Mince the garlic and onion and add them, along with the veal that has been cut in pieces. Cook until the meat and vegetables are nicely browned. Add the wine and 1 cup boiling water to the pan. Toss in the parsley, sprinkle with salt and pepper, and cover the pan. Simmer gently for 1 hour, or until the rabbit and veal are tender. Serves 3–4.

Relleno de Arroz Silvestre (*Wild Rice Dressing*)

This recipe will make enough dressing to stuff four Cornish game hens or one roasting chicken of 3 to 3½ pounds.

1 teaspoon olive oil
¼ pound lean ground beef
2 slices boiled ham
3 tablespoons minced onion
1 clove garlic

2 tablespoons minced parsley
½ cup chopped walnuts
1 hardboiled egg
2 cups cooked wild rice
salt and pepper

Brown the ground beef in hot olive oil. Dice the ham, and add it to the beef along with the onion, garlic (minced), parsley, and walnuts. Stir and cook until the vegetables are barely tender. Remove the pan from the stove. Chop the egg and add it, along with the wild rice. Mix well and season to taste with salt and very little pepper.

Relleno para Pavo (*Stuffing for Turkey*)

Mamá had not been in San Francisco many years before she succumbed to the American custom of roast turkey for Thanksgiving and Christmas dinners. Her dressing recipe is sufficient for a 12-pound bird.

1 tablespoon olive oil
⅓ pound each ground beef,
    veal, and pork
1 large onion
1 clove garlic
1 stalk celery
¼ cup minced parsley

1 cup chopped walnuts
1 cup raisins
1 cup sliced black olives
1 cup diced day-old bread
¼ teaspoon allspice
dry white wine
salt and pepper

Sauté the ground meat in hot olive oil until it is lightly browned. Mince the onion, garlic, and celery, and add these to the meat, cooking until the vegetables are barely tender. Remove the pan from the stove and stir in the walnuts, raisins, olives, bread, and allspice. Moisten slightly with white wine. Season to taste with salt and pepper.

Pescados Y Mariscos (Fish and Shellfish)

Basques hold both fish and shellfish in high regard, and Mamá served one or the other every day.

The same little fish seller stopped at Hotel Español each morning. In the early days he had driven an oilcloth-topped wagon pulled by an aging dappled horse. Mamá thought too many of the horse's ribs showed so she always tucked a carrot or apple in her apron pocket when she heard the clump of hoofs in the alley outside.

Now the horse and wagon were gone. The vendor rolled smoothly to the back door in a shiny blue truck and tooted his horn three times. Mamá missed the old days.

But the fish man always had a good selection, and sometimes he gave Mamá fishheads that she would clean and simmer—with a little garlic, onion, and celery—for soup stock.

Often Papá walked down to Fisherman's Wharf, where fish were displayed on white marble tables in buildings that doubled as storage sheds. One of the buildings had even set aside a corner for small tables and chairs, and Papá liked to stop there for a seafood cocktail and a big bowl of oyster crackers.

Ajo Arriero (Salt Cod, Navarre)

Both the sea and the streams are generous with the Basque country and provide an abundance of fresh fish. It is with some surprise, then, that one discovers that two of the favorite fish dishes are based on dry salt cod. The cod is prepared for market by splitting, salting, and drying. Each piece is approximately three feet long and has the appearance of a fish-shaped pine board. Considerable soaking is necessary to soften the cod, and the cook must meticulously pick out bits of bone and skin. In American markets salt cod is available in pound packages; happily, the bones and skin have already been removed.

Ajo Arriero, freely translated, means "muleteer garlic." No one knows how the dish got its name but all agree that it is excellent.

2 pounds salt cod	½ small can tomato sauce
¼ cup olive oil	1 4-ounce can sliced pimientos
¼ medium onion	salt and white pepper
3 cloves garlic	2 medium potatoes
2 tablespoons minced parsley	

Wash the cod, changing the water three or four times. Soak the fish in cold water overnight. Place it in fresh cold water to cover and allow it to come to a boil. Drain, squeeze out excess water, and shred the fish.

To prepare the sauce, mince the onion and two of the cloves of garlic and simmer them in the oil until they are golden. Stir in the shredded cod, tomato sauce, parsley, and salt and white pepper to taste. Mash the third clove of garlic in a little water and stir this in, too. Cover and allow to simmer for 1 hour. Add the peeled and diced potatoes 30 minutes before the dish is done. The sliced pimientos are added during the last 15 minutes. Serves 4.

145

Bacalao Navarro (*Salt Cod, Navarre Style*)

2 pounds salt cod	¼ cup olive oil
2 medium onions	1 small can tomato sauce
2 cloves garlic	½ cup minced parsley
1 4-ounce can sliced pimientos	½ cup dry white wine

Wash the cod, changing the water three or four times. Soak it overnight in water to cover. Drain. Cut the fish into 2-inch pieces. Place the pieces in cold water to cover, bring to a boil, and drain well.

Chop the onions and garlic and fry them, along with the drained pimientos, in the olive oil. When the vegetables are tender stir in the tomato sauce, parsley, and wine. Cover and simmer over very low heat for 30 minutes. Place the cod in the sauce and simmer, uncovered, 30 to 45 minutes, or until the fish flakes easily. Serves 4.

Mamá usually served *Bacalao Navarro* with boiled potatoes.

Cazuela de Rapé Koxkera (*Casserole of White Fish*)

This was one of Mamá's favorite ways of preparing white fish. "A very old, old recipe," she noted.

2 pounds firm white fish	2 cloves garlic
1 tablespoon flour	1 buffet-size can peas
1 tablespoon olive oil	2 tablespoons parsley
2 medium potatoes	salt and white pepper
¼ medium onion	

Cut the fish in serving-size pieces and dust it lightly with flour. Brown the slices quickly in hot olive oil and arrange in a casserole. Sprinkle with salt and pepper. Peel the potatoes, cut them in rounds, and *lightly* brown them in the same oil. Add the onion and one of the cloves of garlic and continue cooking until the vegetables are almost tender. Place the potato mixture over the fish.

146

Drain the peas, reserving the liquid, and pour the peas over the potatoes and fish.

Wipe any excess fat from the skillet; add ½ cup water, the liquid from the peas, the second clove of garlic—mashed—and the parsley. Bring to a boil and pour into the casserole. Season to taste with salt and pepper.

Place the casserole, uncovered, in a 350° oven for a half-hour or until the fish flakes easily. *Don't* overcook. Serves 4.

Mero al Jerez *(Halibut in Sherry Sauce)*

3 to 4 pounds halibut steaks	½ cup medium dry sherry
2 tablespoons olive oil	¼ cup slivered almonds
1½ teaspoons salt	2 tablespoons minced parsley

Rub a shallow casserole with a little olive oil, place the halibut in the dish, and drizzle on the rest of the olive oil. Sprinkle the almonds, salt, and sherry over the halibut. Place the dish, uncovered, in a 350° oven for 30 minutes, or until the fish flakes easily. Baste from time to time with the sherry. Sprinkle the minced parsley over the dish 5 minutes before taking it from the oven. Serves 6.

Lenguado con Salsa de Naranjas *(Sole with Orange Sauce)*

2 pounds fillet of sole	1½ cups orange juice
2 tablespoons olive oil	1 teaspoon grated orange rind
1 tablespoon butter	½ cup dry white wine
3 tablespoons minced onion	¾ teaspoon salt

Sauté the fish in the oil and butter until it is golden on one side. Turn the fish and add the onion. Cook over moderate heat until the onion is tender. Remove the fish to a platter. Add the remaining ingredients

147

to the pan and simmer for 10 minutes. Carefully return the fish to the sauce and allow it to heat through. Serves 4–6.

Pescado en Salsa Verde (*Fish in Green Sauce*)

    2 pounds halibut or sea bass
    flour
    salt and pepper
    2 tablespoons olive oil

Cut the fish into serving-size pieces and dust with flour, salt, and pepper. Brown quickly in hot olive oil, but do not allow the fish to cook through. Place it in a casserole while you prepare the following sauce:

Salsa Verde (*Green Sauce*)

    4 cloves garlic
    4 tablespoons minced parsley
    1 teaspoon flour
    1½ to 2 cups hot water
    salt and pepper

Mince the garlic with the parsley until it is almost a paste. Gently fry the vegetables in the same oil the fish was browned in. Stir in the flour and allow it to bubble up. Add the hot water. (There should be only enough liquid to barely cover the fish; the exact amount will depend on the dimensions of the casserole.) Cook and stir the sauce until it thickens slightly. Pour the sauce over the fish. Cover and cook slowly for 15 to 20 minutes. Serves 4.

Truchas Navarre (Trout)

4 trout	flour
2 large potatoes	salt and pepper
4 slices Italian prosciutto ham	parsley and lemon wedges for
or boiled ham	garnish
2 tablespoons olive oil	

Clean and wash the trout. Dry them well, season with salt and a little pepper, and set aside while preparing the potatoes.

Peel the potatoes and cut them in ¼-inch rounds. Cut up the ham. Heat the oil in a skillet and fry the potatoes and ham, shaking the pan occasionally, until the potatoes are tender. Arrange the potatoes and ham on a warm serving plate.

Dust the trout with flour and fry in the same oil the potatoes were fried in until the trout is brown on each side and flakes easily. Place the trout on the same dish with the potatoes and ham and garnish with parsley and lemon wedges. Serves 2–4.

Sardinas (Sardines)

Sardines are probably the most popular fresh fish in Basque cuisine. Allow two to four sardines per person. Clean them well and remove their heads. Wash and pat dry with paper towels. Dust the sardines with salt, pepper, and flour; and fry in hot olive oil to which one clove of garlic has been added, until the fish are brown on each side. *Sardinas* are served either hot or cold with a sprinkling of olive oil and vinegar.

149

Salmonada con Ali-oli (Salmon with Garlic Mayonnaise)

2 pounds salmon steaks
1 teaspoon salt
1 tablespoon lemon juice
parsley and lemon wedges for
    garnish

Tie the salmon in cheesecloth. Bring 2 quarts of water to a boil, add
the salt and lemon juice, and drop in the fish. Simmer 6 to 10 minutes,
or until the fish is tender and flakes easily with a fork.

Drain the fish well, remove the cheesecloth, and chill. Garnish
with lemon wedges and parsley, and serve with the following sauce.

Ali-oli (Garlic Mayonnaise)

2 cloves garlic
¾ cup olive oil
1 egg yolk
1 tablespoon lemon juice
½ teaspoon salt

Peel and slice the garlic and mash it to a paste. Gradually beat in the
oil. Beat the egg yolk in a separate bowl and, *drop by drop,* beat in the
garlic oil. Blend in the lemon juice and salt. *Ali-oli* is also excellent with
cold lobster, cracked crab, or prawns. Serves 4.

Calamares Rellenos (Stuffed Squid)

Squid must be fresh and thoroughly cleaned. Most fish markets
will clean the squid for you, which is a blessing, for it is not the most
delightful of tasks. The head, spiny rod, eyes, and outer skin must be
removed. But be sure to specify that you want the ink sacs saved.

150

2 pounds squid	1 raw egg
3 slices boiled ham	salt and pepper
2 hardboiled eggs	1 tablespoon olive oil
1 slice stale bread	

Rinse and dry the squid. Set the ink sacs aside. Cut off the tentacles and mince them with the ham and hardboiled eggs. Moisten the bread with water and squeeze dry. Add the bread and the raw egg to the tentacle-ham-egg mixture and blend well. Season with a little salt and pepper. Fry in olive oil until the stuffing mixture is lightly browned. Stuff the squid, using a teaspoon. Set the stuffed squid aside while you make the sauce.

Salsa (Sauce)

1 tablespoon olive oil	1 small can tomato sauce
1 medium onion	ink sacs from squid
2 cloves garlic	salt and pepper
½ bell pepper	

Mince the onion, garlic, and pepper and cook them in olive oil until they are tender. Add the tomato sauce and the reserved ink that has been passed through a fine sieve with a little water. Season with a pinch each of salt and pepper. Simmer the sauce for 15 minutes.

Place the stuffed squid in the sauce, let come to a boil, reduce heat, cover, and simmer gently for 45 minutes. Serves 4.

Calamares en su Tinta (Squid in Ink Sauce)

2 pounds young squid	½ small can tomato sauce
1 tablespoon olive oil	½ cup dry white wine
2 cloves garlic	1 tablespoon minced parsley
½ medium onion	salt and pepper

Have the squid cleaned and the ink sacs reserved as in the preceding recipe. Slice the squid in rings about ¼-inch thick. Mince the garlic and onion. Strain the ink through a fine sieve with a little water. Place all the ingredients in a casserole, cover, and simmer over low heat for 45 minutes. Serves 4.

Mariscos Vascongados (Mussels, Basque-style)

If no mussels are available, substitute good-sized clams and call the dish *Almejas Vascongadas*.

2 dozen mussels in their shells	2 tablespoons olive oil
¼ cup dry white wine	3 large tomatoes
1 clove garlic	1 slice French bread
several sprigs parsley	salt and pepper

Scrub the mussels well and wash them in several changes of water. Lay them in a heavy pan with the wine, garlic, and parsley. Cover and cook over a high heat for 4 or 5 minutes, or until the shells open. Remove the meat from the shells; strain the juice and reserve it.

Peel and dice the tomatoes and simmer them in olive oil until they are just tender. Dice the bread and add to the tomatoes. Simmer 10 minutes. Add the mussels and some of the reserved juice; season to taste, and heat through. Serves 4.

Almejas Guisadas (Steamed Clams)

4 dozen clams in their shells	½ medium onion
1 tablespoon olive oil	½ cup dry white wine
2 tablespoons minced parsley	½ cup water or clam nectar
4 cloves garlic	salt and pepper

Wash the clams well in several changes of water. Mince the garlic and onion. Place all ingredients in a heavy skillet. (Go easy on the salt and pepper.) Cover, and cook over medium heat for 20 minutes. Shake or stir the skillet occasionally.

To serve, place the clams in individual bowls and pour the juice over them. Thick slices of French bread and a green salad are necessary accompaniments. Serves 6.

Caracoles (Snails)

Fresh snails must be cleaned very thoroughly and then boiled 15 minutes with a little salt, rewashed and drained. It is much easier to buy canned snails that are already cleaned and cooked.

24 to 30 snails and their shells	1 mint leaf
4 slices Italian prosciutto ham or boiled ham	salt and pepper

Mince the snails, ham, and mint leaf. Mix thoroughly and season with a pinch each of salt and pepper. Stuff the shells with the snail mixture and simmer them, covered, for 1 hour in the following sauce:

Salsa (Sauce)

½ medium onion	½ small can tomato sauce
1 clove garlic	½ cup light stock or water
½ bell pepper	1 tablespoon minced parsley
2 tablespoons olive oil	salt and pepper

Mince the onion, garlic, and bell pepper and fry them in olive oil until they are just tender. Stir in the other ingredients and simmer gently for 15 minutes before adding the snails. Serves 4.

153

Guisado de Pescado (*Fish Stew*)

24 clams in their shells	1 medium onion
1 pound sliced squid	2 cloves garlic
½ cup cooked and shelled shrimp	1 bell pepper
	2 medium tomatoes
1 pound fillet of sole or rock cod	2 tablespoons minced parsley
	hot water
2 tablespoons olive oil	salt and pepper

Wash the clams well in several changes of water. Wash the sole and cut it into small pieces. Steam the clams open in a heavy covered skillet with about ¼ cup water. While the clams are steaming, dice the onion, garlic, bell pepper, and tomatoes. Fry the vegetables in olive oil until they are tender. Sprinkle in the parsley. Now place the fish, shellfish, and vegetables in a casserole or kettle. Add just enough hot water to cover and season with a little salt and pepper. Cover and simmer for 45 minutes. Serves 4–6.

Serve *Guisado de Pescado* in deep bowls and be sure to have a big basket of French bread.

Pescados y Mariscos Asados (*Fish and Shellfish Bake*)

Here's a clambake, Cantabrian Coast-style. First make the broth; then layer the fish and shellfish in a 4-quart kettle or casserole, add the broth, and bake. *Pescados y Mariscos Asados* is best served at the table right out of the kettle. Excellent for informal suppers or outdoor dining.

Caldo (*Broth*)

2 fish heads	10 cups water
2 cloves garlic	1 cup dry white wine
pinch of saffron	2 cups bread crumbs
1 bay leaf	salt and pepper

154

Clean the fish heads and put them in a pot with the garlic, saffron, bay leaf, and water. Simmer for 30 minutes. Strain the stock and return it to the pot. Add the wine and bread crumbs and simmer gently an additional half-hour. Season to taste with salt and pepper, and be sure the saffron flavor comes through. It must not be overpowering, but you should be aware that there is saffron in the broth.

2 green onions	their shells
1 tablespoon olive oil	3 to 4 pounds cracked crab
1 large tomato	1½ pounds white fish fillets
2 pounds clams in their shells	2 tablespoons minced parsley
1 pound cooked prawns in	1 clove garlic

Wash the clams well in several changes of water. Chop the onions and simmer them gently in olive oil in a large skillet until they are just tender. Peel and chop the tomato and stir it into the oil, cooking for 2 or 3 minutes. Add the clams, cover, and allow to steam over high heat until the clams have opened. Now, using the same kettle or casserole you will serve from, layer the clams, prawns, and crab—topping them with neat slices of fish. Add the broth; it should half-cover the top layer of fish. Mince the garlic with the parsley and sprinkle these on top. Bake, uncovered, in a 350° oven 25 minutes, or until the fish flakes easily. Serve in big bowls and accompany with lots of French bread, wine, and a tossed green salad. Serves 6–8.

Cangrejo con Salsa de Tomate (Crab in Tomato Sauce)

Every year on the opening day of crab season, Mamá would serve *Cangrejo con Salsa de Tomate*. It was a favorite recipe that she brought from Navarre. Sometimes, when she had cooked for a family in the village of Aoiz, she'd used lobster instead of crab. "*Muy bueno!* But *very* expensive."

2 large crabs, cleaned and cracked	1 small clove garlic
1 tablespoon olive oil	1 2-pound can solid pack tomatoes
1 large onion	½ teaspoon salt

Mince the onion and garlic and brown them carefully in hot oil. Mash the tomatoes and stir them in. Add the crab, season with salt, cover, and simmer gently for 20 minutes. Serves 4.

Salsa Para Cangrejo (Crab Sauce)

This recipe will provide sufficient sauce for two small or one large cracked crab.

2 cloves garlic	¾ teaspoon salt
1 tablespoon parsley	¼ cup olive oil
½ bay leaf	1 tablespoon dry mustard
1 small hot chili pepper	juice of 2 lemons

Chop one clove garlic with the parsley, bay leaf, and chili pepper until they are well-minced. In a mortar, mash the other clove of garlic and the salt to a smooth paste. Add the chopped vegetables and olive oil and stir well. Beat in the mustard. Strain the lemon juice and add it.

Arrange the crab on a serving plate with the body in the center and the legs and claws around. Pour the *Salsa* over the crab and refrigerate 2 to 3 hours before serving.

Salsa para Cangrejo, though not originally intended for this purpose, also makes a marvelous marinade and basting sauce for barbecued spareribs or for chicken.

CHAPTER 9

The Depression

Adizkidegabeko bizitxia auzogabeko eriotza.
Vida sin amigos, muerte sin vecinos.
Life without friends, death without neighbors.

Papá was standing in front of the grocery store next door to Hotel Español talking with Maurice and Ernest Figeac about the price of vegetables. It had dropped so that now Mamá could buy a nice selection —enough to make six gallons of soup—for fifteen cents.

Across the street, on the front of a variety store that had been forced to close, workmen were pasting a billboard. It was all in red, white, and blue with a rather attractive Miss Columbia and the lettering, "Business is Good. Keep it Good. Nothing can stop US."

Maurice said the message must be someone's cruel pipe dream, but Papá thought the last sentence, at least, did have some merit. Then he said good day to his friends and turned back to the hotel.

Sitting at his roll-top desk, Papá began rechecking a pile of bills and receipts against his ledger entries. The columns would not balance out; it was futile to spend more time on them. Wearily, he reached for the new paper from the Wool Growers Association. The headline was black, ominous. It reminded Papá of a death announcement. "Wool prices at New Low: 0.46." That was sixteen cents less than last year when wool had sold for less than half as much as the year he'd become a partner of Mr. Marco.

Papá dropped the paper on the stand that held, along with an accumulation of livestock magazines and newspapers, Marty's college catalogs—their covers now a little faded and dusty.

"Next year," Papá promised the catalogs. "Next year."

He looked out into the bar. For being so crowded, it was strangely silent.

Almost every evening another boarder would return to the hotel, shoulders slumped, the thin severance-pay envelope crumpled in his hand. Some of the men, ashamed that they had been let go, continued to leave every morning as though they really did have jobs. But the ruse would be short-lived. Papá's blue eyes would look into theirs—straight —steady. "So?" And the men would tell Papá the truth.

"Papá, here is the money for this week's rent. But then there is no more. So I think, Papá, maybe Nevada. There are many sheep. Perhaps a job—"

"What does the paper say, Papá? But how, in so great a country, can so many be out of work?"

158

"Do you remember Joaquin—the big lumberman, yes? Today I saw his brother, and he tells me Joaquin put his things in a canvas bag and climbed aboard an empty boxcar. He says many men do this same thing. I was thinking, Papá, if I—as Joaquin—"

So the monologues went. A monotony of hopelessness, bewilderment, and doubt.

Papá, however, had the same firm answer for each man. "Stay. There is no work in Nevada, either. Riding in a boxcar? It would be foolish. Poor Joaquin. He thinks that a powerful arm makes a powerful head. But that is not often true. No, it is best to stay at Hotel Español. You have your room. The kitchen is not bad. Perhaps more bread, more beans and rice. But not bad. Here, a glass of whisky to toast your good decision."

So the boarders stayed. There was never a word about their bills. There were no entries made in Papá's ledger.

❋ ❋

These were hard years—bitter years. No one had anything. Yet, perhaps because of this, they had more; they had each other.

"A Basque," Papá said, "is *casco gorra* (stubborn). These bad times will pass and we must not be broken by them." So Papá was especially careful to make sure that the talk at the bar did not turn to the somber problems of the day. And Mamá in the kitchen did wonderful things with beans or rice and a handful of meat.

Marty caught the spirit of it, too. At night—with Marty in his waiter's uniform, hurrying from table to table, making jokes, or helping Papá at the bar—few were aware that the boy had just put in an eighthour day as a shipping clerk at the Wool Exchange.

And Louise, though twelve was a little young for a waitress, regarded her assignment as a privilege and secretly welcomed the balancing of heavy trays as a respite from her school homework and as a sign of growing up.

Little Benny Bufano, who spent his days carving towering statues, beamed at Louise with his special shy smile. "My little Madonna." Perhaps he had never seen a waitress who was even shorter than he.

So the people who had nothing but each other came more and more to Hotel Español. And here they became like a large family. The sheepherders and wool growers, who had been there first, welcomed the firemen and the firemen's families. The firemen, who could never forget how Mamá brought them kettles of hot soup on the days they fought their worst blazes, welcomed the newspapermen; and they, in turn, welcomed the unemployed artists, the pensioners on tiny stipends, and the couples with too many children and dwindling savings accounts.

There was lovable old Bill Knowlton. Sometime—far in the past— he'd been checkers champion of San Francisco. He would buy Louise maple-nut ice cream at the little shop down the hill and tell her of the beauties of Vermont. Then, before supper (he was a daily diner), he would take his accustomed place at Papá's bar. If he felt that the tone of a discussion was becoming too weighty—that a depressing argument might ensue—he would say a very loud "Tut-tut" emphasized by two taps of his finger. And that was the end of that.

There was Jimmy Hatlo and his fellow cartoonist and pal, Hank Jackson. They would try to outdo each other's drawings on Mamá's white tablecloths and feign alarm under her firm but gentle scoldings.

There was Lefty O'Doul who, when he wasn't managing the San Francisco Seals, amused himself and the rest of Hotel Español with endless card tricks. His antics, and those of the magician whose only name seemed to be "Steve", often had both the bar and the dining room in an uproar. And Steve received more than one of Knowlton's "Tut-tuts" for causing a platter of chicken to disappear or a wine bottle to move out of reach.

There were all these and many more. In those years, the family of Hotel Español was poor, but it was big and happy and growing all the time. "In the heart, all true Basques," said Papá. Mamá smiled and slipped her hand into his.

❊ ❊

Something had always been wrong with the wiring at Hotel Español. If all the downstairs lights were turned on at once, it was more than likely that a fuse would blow and the entire building would be plunged into darkness. Papá had saved the money to have the rewiring done. Then 1929 had come and the wiring money, like Marty's college money . . .

So light failure was a common occurrence. Mamá always kept a big supply of candles on hand, and the diners always looked forward to the break in routine.

One night Marty had just opened a new barrel of wine in the storage closet over the dining room when the lights flickered, dimmed, and went out. He felt his way downstairs, helped distribute candles, then moved from table to table, seeing that glasses were filled and empty plates were removed.

Laughter. Conversation. "Is it raining outside?" "No, no. What makes you ask that?" "The roof is leaking." "Impossible!" "But it is." "Look!" And one diner after another stared ceilingward. From more than a dozen nail holes in the pressed-tin ceiling, red wine was beginning to drip. In no time, some of the droplets turned into little streams.

Louise ran for towels, Marty ran to Papá for help, and the diners nearest the leaks held their glasses above their heads.

"It's good—it's good!" "Here—give me your cup." "No, Louise— not towels. Bring a pitcher!"

Papá and Marty took the stairs on the run. Wine was pouring from a split in the new barrel; the storage closet was awash. Jugs, pitchers, kettles were hauled upstairs and filled. "A wine brigade! A wine brigade!" and the diners hurried to help.

161

When the last of the conglomeration of wine containers was carried downstairs, Papá surveyed the wreckage. "Drink up—drink up—*Osagarria!*" And the friends, already in a party mood, refilled their glasses and *botas* and raised them in a toast. Someone put a record on the phonograph. Mamá sliced more bread and cheese.

There were songs and dancing. There was warmth and good fellowship late into the night.

Habas Y Arroz (Beans and Rice)

No market in the Basque country is without a sizeable section devoted to beans, *garbanzos* (chick peas), and rice. Hundred-pound sacks are propped—one against the other—their tops open to display the variety of legumes and cereals that play so important a part in the Basque diet.

Beans, or the Basque favorite, *garbanzos,* are usually served as a separate course preceding the meat. Plain boiled rice sometimes accompanies meat or fish. More often, rice is cooked with a few vegetables or a little meat or fish and served as a separate course.

At Hotel Español, Mamá served beans or rice at least once a day.

HABAS (Beans)

Garbanzos (Chick peas)

Here is the traditional and basic Basque method of preparing *garbanzos.* The dish is always served hot. It can be the main course with bread, cheese, and a salad. It can be a side dish with meat, fish, or chicken. Leftover *garbanzos* can be added to soups, stews, omelets, or salads. Basques like to pile *garbanzos* on French bread to make a sandwich.

1 pound dried *garbanzos*	1 clove garlic
1 teaspoon salt	1 tablespoon tomato sauce
1 medium onion	1 tablespoon olive oil

Wash the *garbanzos* and put them in a deep kettle with the salt and lukewarm water to cover; soak overnight. In the morning, add more water, if necessary, to cover the *garbanzos*. Bring to a boil; skim off the foam, and repeat two or three times until the water is clear. Mince the onion and garlic and add them, along with the tomato sauce and oil, to the kettle. Cover and simmer gently for 2 hours. Refrain from stirring the pot, but do check to see that there is enough water.

Garbanzos y Chorizo (*Chick Peas and Chorizo*)

4 cups cooked *garbanzos*
  (page 162)
1 pound *chorizo* (pages 126–128)
1 tablespoon minced parsley

Simmer the *chorizo* for 15 minutes to remove excess fat. Drain and cut in small pieces or leave whole. Combine the *chorizo* and *garbanzos* and simmer, covered, for 20 minutes. Sprinkle with parsley before serving. Serves 4.

Alubias Rojas (*Cranberry Beans*)

Cranberry beans, prepared in the Basque way, have a wonderfully meaty flavor, though no meat is added to them.

163

1 pound dry cranberry beans	1 tablespoon olive oil
¼ medium onion	1 tablespoon butter
2 cloves garlic	salt and pepper

Wash the beans and soak them overnight. Drain and add fresh water to top the beans by two inches. Bring to a boil and skim off any foam. Mince the onion and garlic and add, with the oil and butter, to the beans. Season with salt and pepper. Cover and cook slowly for about 1½ hours, or until the beans are tender. Check the pot from time to time to be sure the water has not evaporated. Serves 6.

Alubias Blancas (Navy Beans)

Follow the recipe for *Garbanzos* (page 162) except for three small changes: skip the overnight soaking; use two cloves of garlic; simmer the beans for 1½ to 2 hours. Serves 6.

Alubias Blancas con Jamón (Navy Beans with Ham)

1 pound dry navy beans	1–1½ pounds ham
1 medium onion	½ small can tomato sauce
2 stalks celery	salt and pepper
2 medium carrots	½ pound *chorizo* (pages
1 potato	126–128) and/or blood
2 cloves garlic	sausage (optional)

Cover the beans with cold water, bring to a boil and skim off any foam. Chop the onion, celery, carrots, and garlic. Peel the potato and cut it into large pieces. Add the vegetables to the beans. Drop in the ham. It may be left in one piece, or you can have the butcher saw through the bone and cut the meat, including the rind, into good-sized chunks. Cover the pot and simmer the beans slowly for 1½ hours, or until the beans are tender. Add the tomato sauce during the last half-hour of cooking. Season to taste with salt and pepper. Serves 6–8.

If *chorizo* or blood sausage is used, simmer separately for 15 minutes to remove excess fat. Add to the beans during the last half-hour of cooking.

Lentejas con Tocino (*Lentils with Bacon*)

1 pound dry lentils	2 potatoes
4 carrots	1 pound slab bacon
2 medium onions	salt and pepper
4 stalks celery	

Rinse and drain the lentils, chop the onion and celery, and cut the carrots and potatoes into large pieces. After removing the rind, cut the bacon into six pieces. Put all the ingredients into a large kettle and cover with cold water. Cover and simmer for 1¼ hours, or until the lentils are tender. Check the water occasionally to be sure too much has not evaporated. At the same time, don't add so much water that the final result is soupy. Before serving, season with salt and pepper. Serves 6–8.

Lentejas con Chorizo (*Lentils with Chorizo*)

This is a simple though excellent dish. The seasoning in the *chorizo* flavors the lentils to perfection.

1 pound dried lentils
1 pound *chorizo* (pages 126–128)
salt

Rinse and drain the lentils. Simmer the *chorizo* for 15 minutes and drain. They may be either cut up or left whole. Combine the lentils and *chorizo* in a heavy pan and cover with cold water. Bring to a boil, reduce heat, and simmer—covered—for 1¼ hours, or until the lentils are tender. Season with salt. Check from time to time to be sure too much water has not evaporated. Serves 6–8.

Lentejas con Verduras Fritas
(*Lentils with Fried Vegetables*)

1 pound dry lentils	1 clove garlic
3 slices bacon, ham, or salt pork	1 teaspoon minced parsley
½ medium onion	1 small can tomato sauce
1 stalk celery	salt and pepper

Rinse and drain the lentils, put them in a kettle, cover with cold water, and bring to a boil. In the meantime chop the bacon, onion, celery, and garlic and fry them gently until the bacon is semi-crisp and the vegetables are tender. Stir in the parsley during the last minute or two of frying. Add the bacon-vegetable mixture and the tomato sauce to the lentils, cover the pot, and simmer gently for 1¼ hours or until the lentils are tender. Check from time to time that there is sufficient water. Season to taste before serving. Serves 6–8.

ARROZ (*Rice*)

Hotel Español's diners always looked forward to Mamá's rice. They thought that it was better than any they'd had at home or in other restaurants. It was. They claimed they could eat it every day because it never became monotonous. It didn't. What then, the diners would ponder, was Mamá's secret?

A look into her gleaming kitchen would have told. Mamá simply augmented the water used to cook the rice with a dipperful of soup stock. Sometimes it was beef, sometimes chicken. Or, if she had boiled a tongue, she would use some of that broth instead. Or—especially when the rice was meant to accompany fish—Mamá would add a good squeeze of lemon juice to the water in which the rice was to cook.

"Un poquito. Un poquito (a little)"—she cautioned assistants. "The rice has its own flavor. To hide it would be a shame."

Sometimes, if the rice were to accompany a meat or fish course that was not highly seasoned, Mamá would cook a bit of onion or garlic, a few sliced pimientos, or a sprinkling of parsley with the rice. Her advice, *"Un poquito,"* applied here as well.

But it was Mamá's rice dishes—the knack she had of combining rice with fish, poultry, or meat as a separate course—that brought so many diners to Hotel Español again and again. Among these dishes, the favorite by far was *Arroz con Almejas* (Clams with Rice).

Arroz con Almejas (*Clams with Rice*)

Mamá always insisted on fresh clams for this truly Basque dish; but, if they are unavailable, canned clams may be substituted. Remember, whatever you do, to use only the tiniest pinch of saffron; it is the clam flavor that must dominate.

4 pounds (2½–3 dozen) medium-size clams in their shells	parsley
	pinch of saffron
	1½ cups raw rice
¼ cup olive oil	3 cups boiling water or
¼ medium onion	clam nectar
2 cloves garlic	salt and pepper
1 tablespoon chopped	

Arroz con Almejas should come to the table in the same pan in which it was cooked. A large fireproof earthenware casserole is excellent. Otherwise, use a broad skillet that has a tight-fitting lid.

Wash the unshelled clams well in several changes of water. Mince the onion and garlic and put them into the casserole along with the oil and clams. Cover and allow to steam over high heat until the clams open (approximately 5 minutes). Add the rice and stir for a few minutes until it begins to brown. Sprinkle in the parsley and saffron. Season with a pinch each of salt and pepper and pour in the boiling water. Stir well, bring to a boil, and cover. Lower the heat and simmer for 20 to 30 minutes or until the water is absorbed and the rice is tender. Serves 4.

Although Mamá served *Arroz con Almejas* as a first course (it was usually followed by beans, vegetables or mashed potatoes, and a roast), it makes an excellent main dish accompanied by a green salad, French bread, and wine. It's wonderful for a summer evening when you want to serve an elegant dish without spending hours in a hot kitchen.

Arroz con Costillas de Cerdo (Spareribs with Rice)

This is another excellent dish whose preparation is similar to *Arroz con Almejas.*

4 pounds pork spareribs	pinch of saffron
2 tablespoons olive oil	1 teaspoon parsley
1 clove garlic	1 cup raw rice
¼ onion	2¼ cups boiling water
1 whole clove	salt and pepper

Cut the ribs into serving-size pieces, sprinkle with salt, and brown well in hot oil. Lower the heat and continue to cook the ribs until the outside is crisp and the meat is nearly done. This will take from 30 to 45 minutes.

Drain excess fat from the pan and add the onion and garlic, both finely minced. Shake the pan to cook the vegetables evenly. Now stir in the rice, along with the clove, saffron, parsley, and salt and pepper to taste. Add the boiling water. Bring the rice to a boil and arrange the spareribs on top. Cover the pan and lower the heat. Simmer for 20 to 30 minutes, or until the rice is tender and has absorbed all the moisture. The spareribs should retain their crispness. Serves 4–6.

The Basque way of cooking clams or spareribs with rice can be applied to other fish and meat, and also poultry. And, although the seasoning ingredients are the same, each dish has its own distinctive flavor, making it entirely different from any of the others. Here are some Basque specialties to try. Simply follow the directions for either of the classic rice dishes above.

Arroz con Pollo (Chicken with Rice)

Use two very young split fryers (1¼ to 1½ pounds each), or one 2- to 2½-pound fryer cut in serving-size pieces. Season the chicken with salt and pepper, and fry until the skin is crisp. Then proceed as for *Arroz con Costillas de Cerdo* (page 168). Serves 4.

Arroz con Hígados de Pollo (Chicken Livers and Rice)

Quickly brown 1 pound chicken livers in hot olive oil. (Take only a minute or two for this because chicken livers cook quickly and they will have more than sufficient time as the rice steams.) Season with salt and pepper. Follow the directions for *Arroz con Costillas de Cerdo* (page 168). Serves 4.

169

Arroz con Borreguito (*Lamb Shoulder and Rice*)

Brown 2 pounds lamb shoulder stew meat in hot olive oil. Season with salt and pepper. Then proceed as for *Arroz con Costillas de Cerdo* (page 168). Serves 4.

Arroz con Camarones (*Prawns and Rice*)

Prepare the rice as for *Arroz con Almejas* (page 167). Top the rice with 1 pound cooked shelled prawns just before adding the boiling water and proceeding as for the remainder of the *Arroz con Almejas* recipe. Serves 4.

Arroz Marinero (*Rice with Fish*)

Arroz Marinero is a favorite Lenten dish, but it would be a shame to limit it to that season only. It varies according to what fish and shellfish are available. To prepare it, select two pounds of assorted fish and shellfish (halibut, sole, red snapper, clams, prawns, snails, lobster, squid, etc.). Clean the fish and fry them quickly (only long enough to brown) in hot olive oil. Remove and keep warm. Steam open the shellfish as directed in the recipe for *Arroz con Almejas* (page 167). Return the fried fish to the pan and follow the remaining directions for *Arroz con Almejas*. Serves 4.

Arroz Verde (*Green Rice*)

The ingredients in this rice dish are similar to those for the preceding rice dishes, with slight changes that make a great difference in the final flavor. This method may be used with clams, prawns, chicken fried with a little salt, well-browned spareribs or lamb shoulder, or whole canned pimientos (2 4-ounce cans).

1 clove garlic	1 cup raw rice
3 tablespoons olive oil	2¼ cups boiling water
1 tablespoon minced parsley	salt and pepper
pinch saffron	
2 or 3 tablespoons dry	
white wine	

Mash the garlic with 2 tablespoons of the olive oil, the parsley, saffron, and a pinch of salt and pepper in a mortar until you have a fine paste. Heat the remaining tablespoon of oil in a skillet that has a tight lid. Stir the rice into the oil and stir and fry until each grain is a pale golden color. Pour in the boiling water and quickly stir in the garlic mixture. Rinse the mortar with the wine and add this to the rice. Stir once more. Arrange the clams, fried chicken, browned meat, or pimientos on top and cover immediately. Lower heat and simmer gently for 20 to 30 minutes or until the rice is tender and all the water has been absorbed. Serves 4.

Arroz con Verduras (*Rice with Vegetables*)

This dish goes especially well with fried chicken or with roast veal.

2 tablespoons olive oil	pepper or 1 green bell
1 tablespoon butter	pepper and 1 4-ounce jar
1 cup raw rice	sliced pimientos
2¼ cups hot stock	1 medium onion
1 each green and red bell	salt and pepper

Heat one tablespoon olive oil and the butter until they begin to foam. Add the rice and stir, over medium heat, until the rice is golden. Add the hot stock, bring to a boil, cover, and reduce heat. Simmer for 20 minutes or until the stock is absorbed and the rice is tender.

While the rice is cooking, seed the peppers and chop them. Chop the onion. Simmer the vegetables in one tablespoon olive oil until they are tender. Just before serving toss the vegetables with the rice and season with salt and a little pepper. Serves 4–6.

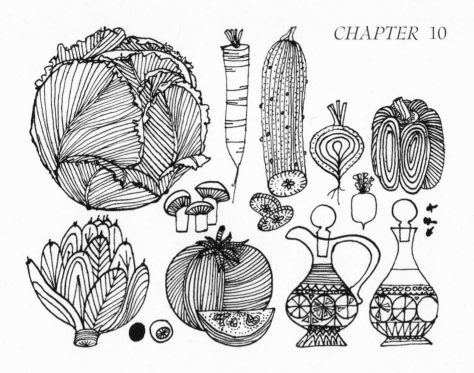

CHAPTER 10

Papá Takes a Trip

Urzo churia, erro zu, norat joaiten ziren zu.
Palomita blanca, dime donde vas.
Little white dove, tell me where you're going.

Papá had always wanted to return to the Basque country. Not to stay, for America was now very much his home. But to visit his family, his friends. To walk again with Mamá in the villages of their childhood —Escay and Gorriz.

But something was forever getting in the way of his intended trip.

173

First, he had spent a lot of money buying sheep. Then he'd made a lot of money, but the Depression . . . (no use dwelling on that). Then his good friend and partner, Santiago, had become so ill that he'd been forced to retire and Papá had taken full charge of Hotel Español.

1936 came and Papá almost went back to Spain (in his heart, at least). Sometimes, during those four terrible years of the Spanish Civil War, Papá had secret thoughts of returning to Navarre. "Brother against brother—" he would shake his head, his lashes glistening with tears. "Perhaps. Perhaps if I . . . " But the very thought that he alone could save all of Spain was so ridiculous that it would shock him from his sad reverie and change his tears to laughter.

1939 brought the Golden Gate International Exposition to Treasure Island in San Francisco Bay. Like any true Basque, Papá loved fairs and fiestas, so when the first plans were announced his enthusiasm needed no encouragement.

Day by day, he followed the Exposition's progress. "Imagine," he told Mamá, "right here in the Bay they are going to build an entire island. There will be exhibits from every land. There will be music and dancing and fireworks. Such a fiesta we have never seen!"

For months before the fair's official opening date, Papá received letters from friends and friends of friends throughout California, in Nevada, and as far away as Washington and Idaho. It looked as though all the Basques in America were coming to San Francisco in 1939.

When the last rooms at Hotel Español had been booked solid, Papá went from hotel to hotel all over San Francisco arranging accommodations for every person who wrote to him.

One day he handed his daughter Louise a pad, a pencil, and a tape and put her to work listing her measurements and those of the four waitresses.

"Why, Papá? Are we—?" But Papá's bright blue eyes silenced her. Without words they clearly stated, "The 'why' is man's work; it is the measuring that is yours."

A week before the Exposition was to open five suit boxes were delivered to Hotel Español, and Papá distributed them to Louise and the waitresses. Each box contained a white blouse with gently puffed sleeves, a laced vest of black velvet, and a full red shirt banded with black stripes. "Now you shall all be true *Vascas.*"

The fair that was to have lasted a year ran on for two, and—as Papá had said—it looked as though all the Basques in America were making the trip to San Francisco. They came from the endless grazing lands, the isolated farm towns, the forests, and the mines. They came to visit the fair, to wonder at Chinatown, to look at the sea lions through the big binoculars at the Cliff House, to sniff the deep crab pots at Fisherman's Wharf, to ride the cable cars and the ferries, and to drive over the new Bay Bridge.

Wherever they went, Papá must go with them. "Perhaps, today, Marty will go with you," Papá sometimes would suggest. "I have the meat to order, a man is bringing a new wine to try, and . . . " "No. No." His friends would not hear of such a thing. "Marty will do all of that. He is young and strong, and he must learn. Marty will stay; you come with us. After all, Papá, this is fiesta! How can you work during fiesta?"

Finally the lights on Treasure Island went out for the last time. The fair was over. The friends went home.

Again Papá made plans to go to Spain. He collected travel folders and timetables and pored over maps. On the morning of December 7, 1941, while the radio was still crackling terse reports about Pearl Harbor, Papá bundled all his travel literature into a newspaper, fastened it with rubber bands, and put it into the bottom drawer of his desk.

For five years any thought of travel was forgotten. Papá, Louise, and Marty, armed with Hotel Español ration stamps, combed the city for the best cuts of meat, the finest cheese, the purest olive oil. Three times a week, coasting his car down the hills to save gas, Marty drove forty miles north to Petaluma where a friend supplied the hotel with hundreds of tender chickens.

175

Mamá did remarkable things with the rationed food, and one would never have known that some supplies were very limited.

Whenever the battleship *Missouri* was anchored in the Bay, thirty to forty of the ship's boys would eat at Hotel Español every day. They never said a word when sailing orders came, but Hotel Español knew. The boys would pin an insignia on each waitress, shyly kiss Mamá on both cheeks, and shake Papá's firm hand. *"Osagarria—Osagarria."* They were gone.

In 1948, Papá again began planning for his trip to Spain. It was a good time. Now that the war was over, running the hotel was not so hectic. Marty, who had been managing the hotel with Papá, could handle things alone. Mamá's brother, Serapio, who had come from Crockett, the little town across the Bay, to help Papá during the war, could assist Marty. Louise was home again, where her baby, Virginia— like Louise herself—had been born. Yes, Louise could take care of the dining room. So, at last, Mamá and he were going.

Papá talked constantly of the wonderful trip to Spain—of how good it would be to see the family again, of how important it was that every Basque make at least one visit to the place of his birth. Everyone listened to the talk. They agreed that it was important to see one's family again. They agreed that a visit to one's birthplace was paramount. They agreed wholeheartedly with everything Papá said. And they began having faraway looks in their eyes.

"Papá," said Serapio one day, wiping the bar thoughtfully. "For many years we have talked about the trip to Spain, and now I have made up my mind. My son Richard finishes his studies at the Sorbonne this summer. He could meet us in Pamplona and together, we could show him the old country—introduce him to his family there. Yes, I will go to Spain with Mamá and you."

Papá was delighted. "So!" he beamed, "What a fine plan! Perhaps young Richard can arrive in time for San Fermín—take part in the *encierro*. Remember, Serapio, how you and I, as boys, would look forward to running in the streets with the bulls . . . ?"

Pedro, Papá's nephew, had been working at Hotel Español for several years. Now he was preparing messages and gifts for Papá and Mamá to take to Navarre. Pedro listened to all the talk. Then, one evening, he wondered aloud if perhaps it might not be good if he, too, went to Spain. Besides, if he went it would really save money, for he and Serapio could share hotel rooms on the way.

"Why not!" agreed Papá. "That is a very good idea. Besides, with you along, if anything goes wrong, I'll have an extra strong helper."

Avelino, the brother-in-law of Papá's old partner, Santiago, heard snatches of this conversation—though most of his time was spent in the kitchen where, since 1934, he had worked side by side with Mamá. Together they shared their cooking secrets: the seasoning of vegetables, the making of mayonnaise. And, while they worked, Mamá talked to Avelino about the trip, wondering how things had changed in the years since each of them had left Navarre.

Avelino decided to join the group going to Spain.

One day a letter written in a fine hand arrived from the little lumber town of Susanville, California. It was from a Mrs. Larrea who said that she had heard about Papá's and Mamá's trip. She, too, was planning a visit to Navarre, but—being a woman, and alone—she wondered . . .

A lady going to Spain alone! Papá would not permit such a thing. He wrote her the very same day, inviting her to join them.

Papá's and Mamá's travel group was now three times its original size. It was time to give some thought to how this many people could be moved from place to place. Papá had decided, somewhere in the planning, that—although they would fly to Madrid and then take a train to Pamplona, Navarre's capital—they must somehow see as much of Spain as they could. He wanted to visit all the big cities, and he wanted to go to France and Italy as well. And, more important, on the return trip Papá must see the United States: the famous buildings, the battle-grounds, the monuments to important people—all the things that had figured in the history of his adopted country.

Papá went to a North Beach automobile dealer and, when he came home, he had a handful of papers and documents that said he had pur-chased a Chrysler New Yorker that would be delivered to him at the dock in Bilbao, Spain—the closest port-city to Pamplona.

"A car! But, Papá, you don't drive!"

"Serapio will drive," Papá stated firmly.

"So much driving will be too hard for Serapio. He will become tired, what if he becomes sick?"

Papá was silent a full minute. "Louise drives." He turned to his daughter. "Louise will go to Spain with us—and little Virginia, of course. Louise, you must buy the baby some new clothes. And a travel suit for yourself. Go—now. And take Mamá. See that she has a nice new dress, too."

So, on June 1, 1949, after two decades of planning, Mamá and Papá were on their way to the Basque country. And with them went Serapio, Pedro, Avelino, Mrs. Larrea, Louise, and baby Virginia.

Papá insisted on carrying all the tickets, passports, health cards, luggage inventories, baggage receipts, and car documents himself. As soon as the plane was off the ground, he pulled down the tray in front of him and began sorting papers. "Look—look! Lake Tahoe!" "Oh, look. How much snow!" "Look!" "Look!"

"Bai—bai," Papá nodded absently—sorting, filing, and rechecking his papers.

The party changed planes in New York and Papá carefully lined up everyone and all their luggage (enough for a four-month visit)—to make sure that no person or thing was missing. Everyone had questions and suggestions—in Basque, Spanish, and English. The porters grabbed at the pile of luggage. The customs men and airlines officials barked requests. Virginia began to cry.

Papá picked up the child. Softly he began to hum. *"Urzo churia, erra zu, norat jualten ziren zu . . . "* He handed the sheaf of tickets and documents to Louise. Without a word, Papá had appointed her his secretary for the remainder of the trip.

Once they were really on their way, Papá could barely wait to reach Navarre. He checked his watch constantly. He asked the stewardess if they were not flying slower than usual. He was first through customs in Lisbon and had his group lined up at the gate marked "Madrid" long before plane time.

It was 1:30 a.m. when they arrived at their hotel in that capital city. "Ah—a bath." "A good sleep." "Some sightseeing." "Evening strolls in Retiro Park." Each had his own ideas on how best to spend the few days they were scheduled to be in Madrid. They sank into the deep chairs in the lobby while Papá went to talk with the concierge. He talked for a long time. There was waving of arms. There was the concierge's voice—words like "Impossible"—"But the roads"—and "Highwaymen." There were telephone calls to make.

Papá had an announcement, and it startled the dozing group wide awake. There was no train to Pamplona for four days. It was a pity, being so close to their relatives after all these years, to waste so much time in Madrid. So—Papá had hired a limousine. It would come at six that very morning. In less than five hours they would be on their way: "Just enough time for a nice rest," Papá announced, and added the warning: "But don't unpack your bags."

Rain was beginning to fall when they straggled out of the hotel at six o'clock sharp. The "limousine" was waiting. It was a vintage station wagon that had seen service in the Spanish Civil War. Its tires were smooth and it listed precariously to the left. Papá supervised the tying of baggage on the luggage rack, putting the heavier suitcases on the

179

right in hopes of better balance. Mamá, Louise, and the baby got into the car. Mrs. Larrea continued to flutter about outside for she had over-heard the word "highwaymen." Yet, if she didn't go now, she would not only have to spend four days alone in Madrid, but go alone on the train. No. *That* she could not do.

Papá pushed Serapio, Pedro, and Avelino into the car and hopped in behind them. *"¡A Pamplona hemos de ir!"* ("To Pamplona we must go!") his voice roared out the old song. The driver ground through several gears.

They were off!

Ensaladas Y Legumbres (Salads and Vegetables)

In the Basque country, vegetables, as salads, are served as a sepa-rate course following the soup. Asparagus tips or artichoke hearts are popular. Sometimes they are served cold with mayonnaise. Or they may be gently simmered in a little olive oil and garlic.

But usually two or three vegetables are cooked together, such as green beans and potatoes or cabbage and potatoes. Or, a vegetable may be simmered with a spoonful of tomato sauce or with bits of ham or *chorizo*. Sometimes there are so many bits of meat that the vegetable course could be a complete meal in itself.

ENSALADAS (Salads)

Ensalada Mezclada (Tossed Salad)

Mamá usually served a tossed green salad of romaine, curly endive, or Boston lettuce. Sometimes she would add a few quartered tomatoes, sweet onion rings, strips of bell pepper, sliced radishes, chopped celery, green or black olives, or sliced hardboiled eggs.

Whatever the combination might be, she tossed the salad with a dressing made of three generous parts olive oil, one part wine vinegar, and salt but no pepper.

Tomates con Ajo (Tomatoes with Garlic)

This was a favorite in late summer when California tomatoes are at their best.

tomatoes
garlic
olive oil
wine vinegar
salt

Slice the tomatoes and arrange them on a plate. Peel and mince the garlic. (Use 1 large clove of garlic for every 3 tomatoes.) Sprinkle the garlic over the tomatoes with a good dash of olive oil and 1 or 2 drops of vinegar. Season with a little salt, but no pepper.

Ensalada de Gambas y Patatas (*Shrimp and Potato Salad*)

1 medium onion
5 boiled potatoes
¼ cup minced parsley
¼ cup wine vinegar
1 envelope garlic salad
    dressing mix
2 tablespoons water

⅔ cup olive oil
1 pound shelled cooked
    shrimp
lettuce, pitted olives, sliced
    cucumbers, and sliced
    avocado for garnish

Chop the onion, peel and dice the potatoes, and place them, along with the parsley, in a bowl. Mince half the shrimp and add them to the potatoes. Combine the salad dressing mix, vinegar, water, and oil. Pour one-third of the dressing over the potatoes and mix well. Pour the remaining dressing over the whole shrimp and marinate them for at least an hour.

To serve, mound the potato salad on a platter and garnish the edges with the whole marinated shrimp, lettuce, olives, cucumbers, and avocado. Serves 6–8.

Mayonesa (*Mayonnaise*)

2 egg yolks
½ teaspoon salt
1 teaspoon lemon juice*
1½ cups olive oil

Have all the ingredients at room temperature. Beat the egg yolks with the salt and lemon juice until the mixture thickens. Add the olive oil *very* slowly—almost drop by drop—mixing constantly.

    * Taste the *mayonesa*. You may prefer more lemon juice and this can be added after all the oil has been beaten in. If Mamá ran out of

lemons she would use vinegar instead, though she never thought the taste was as good.

Mayonesa may separate after a few days, though Mamá found it had less tendency to do this if it was kept in a cool place instead of in the refrigerator. This recipe makes 1¾ cups.

LEGUMBRES *(Vegetables)*

Legumbres a la Vascongada *(Vegetables, Basque-style)*

Green leafy vegetables such as spinach, cabbage, and Swiss chard, as well as a number of other vegetables (cauliflower, green beans, peas, artichoke hearts, etc.), were prepared by this simple and delicious method at Hotel Español:

Fry a whole clove of garlic in a little olive oil, mashing gently to obtain all the flavor. Remove the garlic clove. Toss the vegetables in the hot oil, season with salt and a little pepper, and add a scant amount of boiling water. Simmer, covered, until the vegetables are just tender.

Alcachofas con Jamón *(Artichokes with Ham)*

1 pound frozen artichoke hearts or 2 8-ounce cans artichoke hearts	2 tablespoons olive oil
	2 tablespoons minced onion
	2 teaspoons minced parsley
½ cup finely diced ham	1 clove garlic

If frozen artichoke hearts are used, simmer them with one teaspoon of salt and one lemon slice until they are barely tender. Drain. If canned artichoke hearts are used, drain them before using.

Lightly brown the ham in olive oil. Add the onion, parsley, and

183

the garlic that has been minced. Stir and cook until the onion and garlic are transparent. Add the artichoke hearts, shaking the pan to distribute the ham mixture. Cover and simmer over very low heat for 5 to 10 minutes, or until the artichoke hearts are heated through. Serves 4–6.

Carrotas en Salsa (Carrots in Sauce)

1 pound carrots	pinch of paprika
1 teaspoon butter	1 whole clove
1 teaspoon olive oil	1 teaspoon sugar
1 tablespoon minced onion	1 egg yolk
1 small clove garlic	juice of ½ lemon
1 tablespoon minced parsley	salt and pepper
1 tablespoon flour	

Scrub the carrots and cut them in quarter-inch rounds. Melt the butter and olive oil in a heavy saucepan and add the carrots. Shake the pan to coat the carrots with the butter-oil. Cover and sauté for 5 minutes over low heat, shaking the pan from time to time so that the carrots will not burn. Add the onion, parsley, minced garlic, and flour. Stir and sauté for an additional 5 minutes. Season with paprika, the whole clove, sugar, and a little salt and pepper. Add only enough boiling water to barely cover the vegetables. Cover and simmer until the carrots are tender. Remove the pan from the fire and, just before serving, pour the egg yolk that has been beaten with lemon juice, over the vegetables. Toss well. Serves 4.

Guisantes (Peas)

Although this recipe is designed for fresh peas, frozen peas can certainly be substituted, and it does wonders for canned peas.

184

1 medium onion	peas
2 whole cloves	1 tablespoon flour
1 teaspoon butter	pinch each sugar, thyme, and
2 teaspoons olive oil	paprika
1 pound (3¼ cups) shelled	salt and pepper

Peel the onion and stick the cloves into it. Brown gently in butter and olive oil. Stir in the flour and, when it has bubbled up, add the peas with enough boiling water to half-cover them. Season with sugar, thyme, paprika, salt, and a pinch of pepper. Cover the pot and simmer gently for 5 minutes, or until the peas are tender.

To serve, set the onion in the middle of a bowl and pile the peas around it. Serves 4–6.

Pimientos Asados (*Roast Peppers*)

Pimientos Asados is a Basque favorite. Sometimes Mamá cooked both green and red peppers together, which made an attractive (and excellent) accompaniment for roast chicken or roast lamb.

6 bell peppers
2 tablespoons olive oil
3 small or 1 very large clove
   garlic
salt

Holding each pepper on a fork, char the skins over an open flame. Hold the peppers under running water and rub briskly to remove all the skin. Seed and slice. Peel and mince the garlic and simmer it until golden in olive oil. Add the pepper slices, season with salt; cover, and cook slowly for about 15 minutes, or until the peppers are tender. Serves 4–6.

Pimientos y Cebollas (*Peppers and Onions*)

4 bell peppers	1 small clove garlic
2 medium onions	salt
2 tablespoons olive oil	

Remove the skins from the peppers as directed in *Pimientos Asados* (page 185). Seed and slice them. Cut the onions into thin rings. Mince the garlic. Heat the oil in a skillet, add the vegetables and a little salt. Cover the skillet and cook slowly for 15 to 20 minutes, or until the vegetables are just tender. Stir or shake the pan two or three times during the cooking. Serves 4–6.

Pimientos Rojos (*Red Peppers*)

2 4-ounce cans whole pimientos	1 large clove garlic
	salt
2 teaspoons olive oil	

Mince the garlic and simmer it in olive oil until it is golden. Drain the pimientos, quarter them, and lay them carefully in the pan. Sprinkle with a little salt. Cover the pan and cook over very low heat for 10 minutes. Serves 2–4.

Pimientos y Setas con Perejil (*Pimientos with Mushrooms and Parsley*)

2 small cloves garlic	2 4-ounce cans sliced mushrooms
1 tablespoon olive oil	
2 4-ounce cans sliced pimientos	1 tablespoon minced parsley
	salt

Mince the garlic and fry it golden in the oil. Drain the pimientos and add them along with the mushrooms and a little of the mushroom juice. Sprinkle in the parsley and season with a pinch of salt. Stir to combine the vegetables. Cover and cook over very low heat for 10 minutes. Serves 4.

Patatas Vascongadas (Basque Potatoes)

4 large boiling potatoes	1 whole clove
1 small clove garlic	1 teaspoon tomato sauce
1 slice onion	½ teaspoon salt

Peel the potatoes and cut them in thick slices. Mince the garlic and onion. Put all the ingredients into a saucepan and half-cover with water. Cover, bring to a boil, then lower heat and simmer until the potatoes are tender. Remove the clove before serving. Serves 4–6.

Potatoes prepared in this fashion are delicious. But do use a light hand with the seasonings; their purpose is simply to accent the potato flavor.

Patatas con Salsa de Setas (Potatoes in Mushroom Sauce)

4 medium boiling potatoes	salt
1 tablespoon olive oil	1¼ cups stock or water
1 clove garlic	
2 4-ounce cans sliced mushrooms	

Peel the potatoes and cut them into thick slices. Mince the garlic and cook it in hot olive oil until it is tender. Add the mushrooms and their liquid. Stir in the potatoes and the stock. Season to taste with salt. Cover the pot and bring it to a boil. Lower heat and simmer until the potatoes are tender. Serves 4.

187

Patatas en Salsa Verde (Potatoes in Green Sauce)

5 medium boiling potatoes	3 tablespoons olive oil
1 small onion	1½ cups stock or water
1 clove garlic	½ teaspoon salt
½ cup minced parsley	

Peel the potatoes and cut them into thick slices. Mince the onion and garlic and cook them slowly in olive oil until they are tender. Stir in the parsley. Add the potatoes and the stock. Stir gently. Cover the pot and bring to a boil. Lower heat and simmer until the potatoes are tender. Serves 4–6.

Patatas con Alubias Verdes (Potatoes with Green Beans)

2 pounds green beans
3 medium potatoes
½ medium onion
1 clove garlic
2 tablespoons olive oil
salt and pepper

Cut the beans into inch-long pieces. Peel the potatoes and either slice them or cut them into small balls or cubes. Slice the onion and mince the garlic. Put all the ingredients into a pot with a small amount of water. Cover, bring to a boil, reduce heat and simmer for about 20 minutes, or until vegetables are tender. Serves 4–6.

The green beans can be replaced by fresh or frozen peas, in which case the dish is called *Patatas con Guisantes.* Or, if the potatoes are cooked with diced cabbage (a winter favorite), you have *Patatas con Berza.*

Salsa de Codorniz (Quail Sauce)

Mamá had no end of uses for *Salsa de Codorniz*. Sometimes she served it as a sauce with meat or fish. Sometimes a generous bowl of it appeared on the table as a vegetable course. A dish of *Salsa de Codorniz*, accompanied by French bread, cheese, and sliced cold meat, was one of Papá's favorite late-evening snacks. Mamá would use leftover dabs of the sauce in stews or soups, or add it to green beans or lima beans.

1½ pounds fully ripened
  tomatoes
1 tablespoon olive oil
½ medium onion

1 clove garlic
½ bell pepper
½ small can tomato sauce
salt

Pour boiling water over the tomatoes to loosen their skins. Peel and chop them. Heat the olive oil in a heavy pan. Peel and mince the onion and garlic; seed and finely chop the peppers and simmer them all slowly in olive oil until they are tender. Do not allow them to brown. Stir in the tomatoes and the tomato sauce. Season with a little salt. Cover the pan and simmer slowly for 20 to 30 minutes. If *Salsa de Codorniz* is made early in the season before tomatoes have achieved their full flavor, it may be necessary to add a pinch of sugar. Serves 4–6.

189

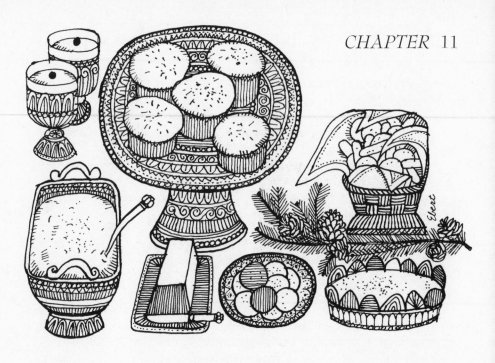

CHAPTER 11

Martin's Español

Nor dabillen bidean arrapatu oi du.
A cada uno le alcanza el comino que anda.
Each reaches the road he walks.

San Francisco! In all of Spain, France, Italy—in the vast reaches of the United States they'd traveled—nothing had looked so good.

They were on the Bay Bridge now, and Papá could see the hands on the Ferry Building clock. "You see," he said elatedly. "It's only midnight, and here we are home. Now, what if we'd stayed in Reno—why we'd have the whole drive to do tomorrow! Wake up! Wake up! We're *home!*"

190

But everyone in the car was awake and had been since they'd left Salt Lake City. Their eyes might be glassy, their minds dull, but there'd been no chance for even the briefest nap. "The last day of our trip!" Papá had boomed as he hustled his traveling group into the car at dawn. "Eyes bright, now. Don't miss a thing!"

And no one had. Papá had seen to that, busily pointing out every object, of historical interest or not, along the way. They'd waded in Great Salt Lake . . . stopped in Lovelock, Nevada, to deliver a message from the Basque country . . . halted from time to time to look at sheep and wave "hello" to the herders . . . and gazed in awe at the statue commemorating the Donner party. Too, there had been the numerous brief stops so Papá could rotate his three drivers: Serapio, Richard, and Louise.

Now the long-awaited trip was over. The car rolled along the Embarcadero and swung up Broadway with Papá giving a running account of his first days in San Francisco and the changes he had seen.

"One more block—look awake, now . . . " Papá's voice stopped in mid-sentence and his mouth stayed open. They were across the street from the hotel, but something was very, very unfamiliar. Where, for the past thirty years, the unobtrusively neat sign "Hotel Español" had hung there was a new sign—many times larger and accented in bright red and yellow neon: "MARTIN'S ESPAÑOL."

For the first time in the entire trip Papá was speechless.

Marty bounded from behind the bar as they stumbled into the hotel. "Surprise, surprise! Did you see the sign, Papá? Do you like it? It's your welcome-home present! I had new menus made and book matches, too. See. Do you like them, Papá?"

Papá gave Marty a warm hug. "Yes, yes. Very nice," he said. "A very nice surprise, Marty. Now, pour us each a little cognac before we go to bed." Papá never said another word about the sign, the menus, the matches, or the fact that the old Hotel Español now bore a new name—Papá's name—in brilliant neon lights.

191

At six o'clock the next morning Mamá was in the kitchen preparing breakfast. Papá, in his usual white apron, was checking the bar receipts. And, except for the fact that the hotel was now Martin's Español, everything was much as it had been on any other morning since 1917.

Except that Papá and Mamá seemed ever busier. The old friends continued to come, many now with graying hair and lined faces. "Papá, do you remember during the bad times of the Depression . . . ? Well, now I have a little farm near Fresno. The land has been good to me, so I come to San Francisco to pay my old bill. *Milesker,* Papá—*milesker!*" ("A thousand thanks, Papá—a thousand thanks!")

A young man or a young woman would arrive, smiling shyly. "Papá, do you know who I am? It was you who took my mother to the hospital when I was born, and Mamá who took care of me. This—this is my first home, Papá."

Or whole families of three generations would come, line up in front of the bar and beam fondly at Papá. And Papá, the patriarch, would survey the group with obvious pride.

There were new friends, too. Broadway had changed since the war—it was, in fact, changing rapidly all the time. More bars, more nightclubs, more bright lights and brassy music. Many who came for the nightlife stumbled onto Martin's Español. Here they found a kind of nightlife they had little expected—an honest friendliness they hadn't discovered elsewhere. They welcomed the good drinks and excellent food, and they respected and learned to love the gentle-but-firm man behind the bar whose blue eyes would look deep into theirs. "No, no, not another drink. Go now and have a big dish of soup and see what else Mamá has prepared for supper." "Yes, Papá." There was a feeling of warmth far beyond any that could be induced by whisky or wine.

* *

Soon it was 1950—and Papá's seventieth birthday. Mamá had made great bowls of floating island and little almond cookies, Louise had put fresh flowers on all the tables, and Marty had given the entire bar a special polishing. Friends were beginning to arrive with birthday cards and boxes of cigars. But where was Papá? He'd gone out several hours before, looking very mysterious and evading any questions. It was time he was home.

Now there was much honking in front of the hotel, and Marty, along with several of the friends, went to investigate. There in the loading zone was the still-shiny Chrysler that had borne Papá's traveling group through Spain, France, Italy, and the United States. And there in the driver's seat, his fingers rapping a lively tattoo on the horn, sat Papá!

Everyone ran to the car and all began talking at once. Marty called Louise and Louise called Mamá. Avelino ran outside too, and so did the waitresses and the friends who had at first remained at the bar.

"Papá—Papá! How did the car get in the street?" "What are you doing in the driver's seat, Papá?" "What?" "Where?" "Why . . . ?"

Papá's eyes were merrier than ever. He gave the horn two final toots, slipped the car in gear, and drove smoothly down Broadway, around the corner, and into the alley. Still without a word he walked through the hotel. Then he reached into his wallet, drew out a driving-school diploma and a brand new driver's license dated that very day, and smoothed them out carefully on the bar for all to see.

❈ ❈

Another year passed. And one morning Papá was standing in front of the hotel—as he loved to do—watching the hurrying autos and pedestrians and listening to the warning clang of the streetcars as they rattled to the crossing.

193

But on this morning he was oblivious to all this activity. He held a letter in his hand and, though its arrival was no surprise, there was something very final in seeing the notice neatly typed under the official letterhead bearing the seal of the City of San Francisco.

Martin's Español was going to be torn down!

Papá had known for over a year that the City planned to build a huge housing project at the north end of Chinatown. And he agreed that there was a definite need. But, at the same time, he wondered why the project could not be a little more to the left—or a little more to the right—*anywhere*, except exactly where Martin's Español stood.

Now the City had made it official: the old wood-frame hotel and the familiar shops that had been its neighbors for so many years would soon be no more.

Where would they go? What would they do? Papá folded the letter and slipped it back into its envelope. There were several alternatives, no one of which seemed right.

Papá could move his hotel to a different part of the City. (But leave Broadway? No, he could never bring himself to do that!) Or—he could relocate the restaurant and bar in a vacant building two blocks down the hill on the other side of the street. There, the bar and dining areas were larger than those in the present hotel—and this was good. But, though there were rooms upstairs, they could not be used for dwelling. This meant there would be no rooms for the boarders. No rooms for out-of-town friends. And, even worse, he and Mamá could no longer live in their own hotel.

Papá mulled over the problem for a long time, then he reached this decision: He would buy a home in the Marina—but the Español must stay on Broadway. Even though it offered no hotel accommodations, the building down the street was the only answer for the restaurant. So there it would move.

Only this time moving was not the one-day affair it had been when

194

Papá had opened Hotel Español forty-one years earlier. For now everything had to go or be demolished by the wreckers. Sadly, Papá announced that Martin's Español would be closed for a month.

Back and forth across Broadway shuttled Papá, Mamá, Louise, and her husband, Gus, and a host of moving men. Mamá's stove and refrigerator were set in place. A chopping-block table, made for her by a carpenter friend back in the days of La Vaporina, was lugged to the new restaurant. The myriad pots and pans, the heavy skillets and kettles, the china and cutlery—all were carefully packed and put in the hands of the movers.

The day the bar was to be moved, Papá was up early and, when the crew arrived with a crane, he gave both the men and their equipment a thorough inspection. "Forty-one years," he said meaningfully. "Forty-one years and not one alcohol ring—not one cigarette burn." His hand stroked the warm mahogany, the bright brass inlays. And his eyes looked piercingly into those of the workmen, clearly telling them that he expected not the tiniest scratch in today's move.

Papá's roll-top desk was trundled to the new restaurant. And Gus personally carried the mounted bull's head that had been given to Papá years before by a Basque sailor and had somehow acquired the distinguished name "Harrison."

Mamá had the five seaman's trunks brought up from the basement. She could barely remember the men who had trustingly stored them with Papá when he had owned La Vaporina. As she had done every year, Mamá aired the contents and put a handful of moth balls in each trunk. Louise suggested that the trunks be left for salvage, but Mamá would not hear of such a thing. "They are not ours to give away or leave behind, Louise. Those good sailors have left them in Papá's care. As you say, the men may never return—but, if they do, they have a right to their possessions." Mamá's gentle voice was unusually stern.

At last everything was moved and in place. The refrigerator and

195

storage bins were restocked. And on December 17, 1958, just a week before Christmas, Martin's Español opened the doors of its new home.

Martin's Christmas Eve party had become a tradition. No one remembered exactly when or how it had started, but everyone looked forward to it and began reminding Papá as early as Thanksgiving Day.

So this Christmas Eve—as always—there was a party. Mamá heaped trays with ham sandwiches and cheese. She sliced *panetone* from the nearby Italian bakery. She arranged bowls of *mazapan* and *turron* and fruit. There were chestnuts to roast.

Preparing the refreshments for the Christmas party always made Mamá think of the past. Of the long-ago days in Gorriz where, not Christmas, but the Feast of Epiphany was the festive time. She remembered that, as a little girl, she'd carefully filled her shoes with clean straw for Los Santos Reyes' camels and had set them just outside the front door. In the morning the straw was always gone and there, in its place, was a sprinkling of nuts and candies—perhaps a bright orange. She'd told Marty and Louise the story of Los Santos Reyes and, throughout their childhood, they had managed to find bits of straw or grass to fill their shoes which they set on a windowsill two stories above San Francisco's busy Broadway.

Christmas also reminded Mamá of dear friends. Particularly, Professor Twining. He'd lived to be nearly a hundred and, during his last forty years, had eaten at the hotel every day. Always at Christmas he'd brought Mama the packages of plum puddings and fruit cakes that his sisters made for him and sent all the way from England. And Mamá had proudly served these alongside the Basque refreshments.

Yes, Christmas was a time for memories and merrymaking.

The party at the new Español was now in full swing. The accordionist was indefatigable—his forehead glistened, and his face was flushed rosy red. Everyone knew the words to the music and the young people, many in Basque dress, had pushed back the tables to dance the *jota*.

Mamá sat happily in her familiar kitchen where she enjoyed

196

watching the merriment from afar. But soon, as invariably happened, someone dashed through the door, caught her by both hands, and pulled her into the midst of the party. "A toast! A toast!" Papá moved close to Mamá. And, together, they looked with love at their family and friends whose glasses were raised to them. *"Feliz Navidad, Papá y Mamá!"* *"Feliz Navidad!"*

Postres Y Bebidas (Desserts and Beverages)

Basques, especially the men, usually prefer only fruit or cheese for dessert. This is not surprising when one remembers that a typical Basque meal begins with appetizers; continues on through soup, vegetables, fish, and meat courses—usually accompanied by wine; and eventually ends with a small cup of coffee and a glass of brandy.

However, sweets are consumed in great quantity. Pastries are a popular late-afternoon snack. Five o'clock in a Basque town finds the cafes crowded—each little table piled high with cakes, *churros* (page 203), or meringues (page 199), served with ice cream, hot chocolate, or soft drinks. The same scene is repeated near midnight.

Basque custards and creams are excellent and, if a dessert is served, it will most often be one of these. There is, you will notice, a heavy use of eggs—especially yolks. Save the leftover whites (they keep well either refrigerated or frozen) for omelets or scrambled eggs. Or they may be used to make *Merengues* (page 204) or *Almendrados* (page 205).

197

Natilla (*Egg Custard*)

6 eggs	1 cinnamon stick
1 cup sugar	¼ teaspoon salt
1 quart milk	

Separate the yolks and whites and set the latter aside. Beat the yolks until they are lemon-color, then slowly and thoroughly beat in the sugar. Bring milk to a boil in a saucepan and set it aside to cool slightly. Slowly blend the egg-sugar mixture with the milk. Add the cinnamon stick and salt.

Cook the custard mixture in the top part of a double boiler over hot, not boiling, water until the custard is thick enough to coat a spoon. Remove the cinnamon stick. Pour the *Natilla* into a large bowl or individual serving cups. Cool and chill. Serves 6.

Usually Mamá beat the egg whites with a little additional sugar and pinch of salt and arranged them on top of the *Natilla*. Or the whites can be held in the refrigerator or freezer and used later for omelets or desserts calling for egg whites.

Crema Española (*Spanish Cream*)

Crema (*Cream*)

6 egg yolks	¼ teaspoon salt
⅓ cup sugar	3 cups milk
½ teaspoon vanilla	1 teaspoon unflavored gelatin

198

Beat the egg yolks until they are thick, and slowly beat in the sugar and salt. Heat the milk in the top part of a double boiler. Beat a little of the hot milk into the egg-sugar mixture and then carefully add this to the milk, stirring all the time. Cook and stir the cream over hot, not boiling, water until the mixture thickens enough to coat a spoon. Now stir in the gelatin that has been dissolved in a little milk, and add the vanilla. Pour the *Crema* into a large serving dish or individual cups to cool.

Merengue (*Meringue*)

6 egg whites
2 tablespoons sugar
pinch of salt
1 cup milk

Beat the egg whites in a bowl until they hold stiff peaks. Beat in the sugar and salt. Bring one cup milk to a boil and slowly pour it over the beaten egg whites. Invert the bowl over a colander to drain excess milk. Place the egg white topping on the custard. Serve *Crema Española* chilled. Serves 6.

For a special treat Mamá would drizzle a caramel topping over the egg whites. She made the topping by melting 1 cup sugar in a heavy skillet until the sugar turned into a golden-brown liquid.

Flan (*Caramel Custard*)

1¼ cups sugar	1½ teaspoons vanilla
6 eggs	¼ teaspoon salt
1 quart milk	

Caramelize ¾ cup sugar by heating it slowly in a heavy skillet until it has melted and turned golden brown. Coat the inside of a baking dish with the caramel. Beat the eggs until they are thick and lemon-colored and carefully blend in the remaining sugar. Beat the milk into the egg-sugar mixture slowly, and stir in the vanilla and salt. Pass the mixture through a fine sieve to assure a smooth custard. Pour the custard into the prepared baking dish. Place the baking dish in a pan of hot water in a 325° oven for about 1 hour. When a toothpick inserted in the custard comes out clean, the *Flan* is done. Cool and chill. To serve, run a thin knife blade around the edge of the baking dish and invert the *Flan* on a deep serving plate. Serves 6.

Arroz con Leché (Rice Custard)

1½ to 2 quarts milk
2 eggs
1 cup raw rice
½ cup sugar
1 teaspoon vanilla
½ cinnamon stick
½ teaspoon salt

Beat the eggs and 1½ quarts milk. Heat them in a saucepan and, when it begins to boil, slowly stir in the rice. Add the sugar, vanilla, cinnamon stick, and salt. Lower the heat so that the contents continue to simmer slowly. Continue stirring. This is one dish that can't be left to tend to itself. If the custard becomes too thick before the rice is tender (about 1 hour) stir in more milk, a little at a time.

When the rice is tender and the liquid is the consistency of a thin custard, remove the cinnamon stick and pour the *Arroz con Leche* into a serving dish. It may be served warm or chilled. Don't overcook—the custard will thicken as it cools. Serves 8.

Isla Flotante Vasca (Basque Floating Island)

Crema (Cream)

1 quart milk	1 teaspoon vanilla
1 tablespoon cornstarch	½ teaspoon lemon juice
½ cup sugar	salt
4 egg yolks	

Bring the milk to a boil. Remove it from the stove and gradually stir in the cornstarch, which has been dissolved in a little water and about ¼ cup of the hot milk. Stir in the sugar. Beat the egg yolks until creamy. Stir about ½ cup of the hot milk into the yolks and then gradually stir this into the above mixture. Add the vanilla, lemon juice, and salt.

Cook and stir the custard in the top part of a double boiler over hot, not boiling, water until it is glossy and thick. Pour it into a serving dish to cool.

Islas (Islands)

4 egg whites
5 teaspoons sugar
vanilla or almond extract

Beat the egg whites until they are stiff, adding the sugar, a teaspoonful at a time. Flavor with a drop or two of vanilla or almond extract.

Pour about an inch of boiling water into a baking pan. Make "islands" by placing the egg white on the water, a tablespoon at a time. Slip the pan into a very slow oven (250°) for 5 minutes or until a toothpick inserted in the "islands" will come out clean. Arrange the "islands" on the custard. Chill before serving. Serves 6.

Bizcochada (Custard with Lady Fingers)

1 quart milk	¼ teaspoon salt
6 egg yolks	1 teaspoon vanilla
½ cup sugar	12 lady fingers

Allow the milk to come to a boil. In the meantime beat the egg yolks well, add the sugar and salt, and continue beating until the mixture is thick and lemon-colored. Slowly stir the milk into the egg yolks. Flavor with vanilla. Cook and stir over hot, not boiling, water until the mixture will coat a spoon. Pour the custard into a serving bowl around which split lady fingers have been arranged. Chill before serving. Serves 6–8.

Torrejas (French Toast, Basque Style)

This is a simple and very good Basque dessert. Though similar to French toast, *Torrejas* are lightly crisp on the outside with custard-like centers.

1 quart milk	3 eggs
1 cinnamon stick	flour
⅓ cup sugar	oil or butter
12 slices day-old white bread	cinnamon and sugar
or thin French bread slices	jelly

Combine the milk, sugar, and cinnamon stick. Bring to a boil and simmer until slightly thickened. Allow the milk to cool. Beat the eggs until they are creamy. Have the flour and bread at hand. Heat the oil in a skillet.

Dip the bread slices quickly into the milk mixture, dust with flour, then dip into the eggs. Fry until golden on each side. Serve immediately with cinnamon and sugar or jelly. Serves 6.

Causerras (*Easter Doughnuts*)

Easter is an important Basque holiday and calls, of course, for special food. *Causerras* are extra-special.

These doughnuts must be eaten immediately. So, if you don't have a large family, invite friends.

1 cup water	pinch of salt
¼ pound butter	1 cup flour
2 whole cloves	8 eggs
1 1-inch piece dried orange peel	shortening for deep-frying
	granulated sugar

Combine the water, butter, cloves, orange peel, and salt in a saucepan. Bring to a boil and allow the butter to melt. Remove the cloves and peel. Keep the pan over a low heat.

Sift 1 cup of flour and quickly beat it into the water-butter mixture. Cook, stirring, until the mixture leaves the sides of the pan. Remove and cool for a minute. Add the eggs, one at a time, beating with a spoon after each addition. Beat *well*. Drop the batter, a tablespoonful at a time, into hot shortening (375°). Fry until golden on one side, then turn to brown the other. Drain on paper towels, sprinkle with granulated sugar, and serve at once. Makes approximately 3 dozen.

Churros (*Basque Crullers*)

Churros are served for breakfast in the Basque country, or as a snack with afternoon coffee or chocolate. During fiestas, portable *churro* stands, complete with bowls of batter and kettles of hot fat, pop up on the busiest street corners. *Churros* should be eaten while they are still warm, for they tend to become limp if left to stand too long.

1 cup flour	1 egg
½ teaspoon salt	shortening for deep fat frying
1 cup boiling water	granulated sugar

Sift the flour and salt into a mixing bowl. Add 1 cup boiling water and beat thoroughly. Add the egg and continue beating until the batter is smooth and glossy. Pour the batter into a pastry tube with a medium-size star tip. Squeeze four-inch or five-inch lengths of batter into hot fat (375°) and fry until both sides are golden-brown. Drain on crumpled paper towels and dust sparingly with granulated sugar. Makes approximately 2 dozen.

Merengues (Meringues)

3 egg whites
¾ cup sugar
¼ teaspoon salt
¼ teaspoon vanilla

Be sure the egg whites are at room temperature. Beat them until they hold stiff peaks, then beat in the sugar, a teaspoonful at a time. Finally beat in the salt and vanilla.

Place spoonfuls of *merengue* on a baking sheet, or use a pastry bag to make fancier shapes. Bake the *merengues* in a 225° oven for 45 to 60 minutes. Remove and cool.

Drizzle caramelized sugar over the *merengues* or serve them with fruit or ice cream.

Almendrados (Almond Cookies)

2 cups blanched almonds
1 cup sugar
2 egg whites
pinch of salt

Grind the almonds to a flour and blend in the sugar. Beat 2 egg whites until they hold stiff peaks. Fold the almond-sugar mixture into the whites along with a pinch of salt. Place spoonfuls of the dough on an oiled baking sheet. Bake for 10 to 12 minutes in a 375° oven. Makes approximately 3 dozen.

Mazapan (Marzipan)

1 pound almonds
1 pound sugar
⅔ cup water
drop of vanilla or orange-
   flower water
6 sugar cubes

Put the almonds through a meat grinder. If you blanch them first the *mazapan* will be bisque-color. Or leave the skins on for a darker and heartier-flavored sweet.

Combine the ground almonds, sugar, and water in a pan and cook and stir to the soft ball stage (250°). Add the vanilla or orange-flower water and stir to blend. Turn the mixture out on a board and, as soon as it is cool enough to handle, knead it thoroughly. Roll the paste about ½-inch thick and cut it into squares or diamonds. Crush the sugar cubes with a rolling pin and sprinkle this coarse sugar over the *mazapan*. Wrap each piece separately in waxed paper and store in a tightly covered container. *Mazapan* is best if it is allowed to ripen 2 or 3 days before serving.

Membrillo (Quince Sweet)

Membrillo is a thick, sugary quince jam made into a loaf. It is sliced and served with cheese.

3 pounds ripe quinces
sugar
salt
1 package fruit pectin

Wash the quinces, remove the blossom ends, and cut them into small pieces. Put them into a heavy kettle with half as much water as fruit. Cook until soft, stirring constantly. Press through a fine sieve.

Measure the sieved pulp and return it to the kettle. Stir in as much sugar as there is fruit, the pectin, and pinch of salt.

The *membrillo* must be allowed to cook slowly until it is nearly firm. Basque cooks usually prepare *membrillo* on top of the stove over very low heat. Then stir and stir, until the mixture is so stiff that it is an effort to move the spoon. An easier method that offers equally excellent results is to place the kettle in a 300° oven and bake the *membrillo* until it is stiff. It must be stirred occasionally.

When the *membrillo* has the right consistency, pat it into a lightly oiled loaf pan. Allow it to cool completely before turning it out of the pan. Wrap in wax paper to store. The flavor of *membrillo* is improved if it is allowed to mellow 5 days before serving.

Castañas (Roast Chestnuts)

Castañas are a treat that Basques reserve for the Christmas season. Mamá would order chestnuts by the sack and roast some almost every day between Christmas Eve and the Feast of Epiphany.

Using a sharp pointed knife, cut a cross in the flat side of each chestnut. Sprinkle a baking pan liberally with salt and place the chestnuts in the pan, one layer deep. Sprinkle the chestnuts with a little water. Place the pan in a preheated 375° oven and roast for approximately 1 hour or until the shells and skins can be removed easily and the nut meat is soft. Serve the chestnuts while they are hot, leaving them in their shells so each person may peel his own.

If it is not possible to serve the chestnuts immediately, wrap them loosely in foil and hold them in the oven with the heat turned off.

Pastel de Navidad (Christmas Nut Cups)

pastry sufficient for 3 pie shells
15 eggs
  2 cups sugar
  2 cubes butter (½ pound)

3 cups chopped walnuts
2 cups raisins
½ teaspoon salt
3 teaspoons vanilla

Roll the pastry as thin as possible and cut in circles big enough to put in muffin tins. Line each muffin cup with the pastry.

Beat the eggs until they are light and beat in the sugar. Melt the butter and beat it into the egg-sugar mixture. Stir in the other ingredients. Fill each cup about three-fourths full. (When filling the shells stir the nut-raisin mixture often, for it tends to settle and you don't want all eggs in one cup and all nuts and raisins in another.) Bake the filled cups 20 to 25 minutes at 375°. Makes 24–36 cups.

BEBIDAS (Beverages)

Wine is the universal Basque beverage. Dry wines (usually red) are served before and during dinner and supper. Sometimes the glass is half-filled with wine and then topped with carbonated water. Sweet wines, such as sherry and muscatel, are served with mid-morning or mid-afternoon cookies and cakes. Brandies, especially one highly flavored with aniseed, accompany fresh fruit desserts.

Men often have a small glass of whisky before meals. There are no cocktails as such, but a light aperitif, vermouth and bitters, is gaining popularity in the Basque country.

Breakfast invariably includes a large cup of *café con leche* or *chocolate*.

Café con Leche (Coffee with Milk)

Perhaps it was during the Arab invasions that the Basques first learned to drink coffee. But, whatever its beginnings, coffee is an important part of the daily diet. And, when a quantity of milk is added, coffee turns into a real food.

1 part double-strength coffee
1 part rich milk

While the coffee is brewing, bring the milk to the boiling point in a saucepan. Pour equal parts of coffee and milk into each cup.

Chocolate Vascongado (Basque Chocolate)

Cortez, who reported that Montezuma II drank fifty jars of chocolate a day, is credited with introducing the cacao bean to Spain. From there it moved to the rest of Europe and, for years, was known as "an excellent West Indian drink."

Basque hot chocolate is rich and decidedly thick. One cup of it for breakfast, along with a slice of bread or a few *churros,* will provide energy for the long hours that will pass until dinner is served.

208

½ pound bar bittersweet
  chocolate
1 quart rich milk
2 teaspoons flour

Break the chocolate into small pieces in a saucepan. Add the milk, blend in the flour, and bring just to the boiling point (but do not allow it to boil), stirring often. Lower the heat and cook and stir until all the chocolate is melted. Do not try to hurry the making of *Chocolate Vascongado;* once the chocolate pieces have melted, the secret is to allow the beverage to thicken. Serves 4.

CHAPTER 12

Osagarria!

1965. It was like any other July in San Francisco: three days of heat alternating with three of fog.

Papá thought that he had not been feeling as well as he should. The heat made him lightheaded and the fog, that cooling blanket he'd always welcomed in the past, chilled him and made him shiver. This morning his chest felt strange and tight—perhaps he was worrying too much about Mamá lately—dear Angelita, she had never fully regained her strength after a bout with pneumonia she'd had early that year. Papá wished he did not have to go down to the hotel—that he could stay home all day with Mamá. He called her name and started down the hall.

Mamá was in the doorway and, for an instant, Papá saw her, but then her face seemed to blur and spin. He heard her voice—so familiar—yet now, somehow, unidentifiable. He felt her warm arms around him.

Days became weeks and weeks became months. Each friend who came to Martin's Español asked about Papá. They tried to reassure Louise, Gus, and Marty with stories they'd heard of stroke victims making miraculous recoveries. They tried to reassure themselves.

They were deeply concerned, too, for Mamá's well-being, and their hearts went out to this little woman who now sat every day by Papá's hospital bed, quietly clasping his worn hand in hers.

For, deep down, everyone knew that Papá would not be able to come back to the hotel. And Martin's Español? How could it go on without either Mamá or Papá who—together—were really the heart of the place?

Then Gus put a notice in the window next to the "Closed Tuesdays" sign. It stated simply: "Closing Business March 27, 1966."

All the friends came. They were sad—and self-conscious at first. But they searched, as is the Basque way, to find some opportunity to turn the evening away from the heartbreak that Papá and Mamá were no longer at the hotel—that Martin's Español was closing forever.

"Osagarria!" Someone began to toast. *"Osagarria!"* Hesitantly at first, other voices joined in.

Glasses were lifted. Platters were passed. Talk, even a bit of song, a few smiles, tears, against the familiar clatter of cutlery. For a little while that evening one could almost imagine that Mamá was there in her accustomed place in the kitchen and that Papá was back, walking among his friends, seeing to it that plates were never empty, glasses were always full.

Papá had taught them, and they tried very hard now to remember his lesson: that when Basques come together, it is not a time for melancholy discussion, sad reverie.

No, at Martin's Español, it was always *"Osagarria!"*—"Good Life!"

211

Index

* *

INDEX

217